A CIP catalogue of this book is available from the National Library of Australia.

Liu, Sarah

500 Words of Wisdom:
From Australia's Most Iconic Women in Business on Success and Leadership
ISBN: 978-0-9808097-7-0

Published by Sarah Liu, Little Girl Big Dream
littlegirlbigdream.com

Published in association with The Messenger Group

The Messenger Group
Design: Edith Swan
Copy Editors: Kate Creevey and Renate Ruge

Published by The Messenger Group Pty Ltd
PO Box H241
Australia Square NSW 1215
www.themessengergroup.com.au

WORDS OF WISDOM

From Australia's Most Iconic Women in Business on Success and Leadership

BROUGHT TO YOU BY SARAH LIU,
FOUNDER AND DIRECTOR OF
LITTLE GIRL BIG DREAM

DEDICATED TO:

Mum and Dad, all my loved ones and our amazing JC
– thank you for all your support, encouragement
and words of wisdom.

All the incredible women who have contributed
and made this possible – you are my inspiration.

Anyone out there with a dream of your own
– this is for you.

CONTENTS

Image courtesy of kikki K

Preface

Contributors

Testimonials

Sarah Liu

Founder and Director, Little Girl Big Dream

THIS WAS A DREAM WITHIN A DREAM.

Some say the best ideas are generated at the most unexpected times. For me, good ideas almost always come to me when I am in bed and on the verge of falling into deep sleep. I still vividly remember the night when the idea of *500 Words of Wisdom* popped into my head. The more I rolled around in bed thinking about it, the more it made me wide awake and my blood start to pump. In the end, I had no choice but to jump out of bed at 2am in the morning and jot down my thoughts about how I was going to make this happen.

As Little Girl Big Dream moves into the third year since its launch, I wanted to take our movement of empowering young women to another level by creating something with a lasting impact. This book was the answer, a resource that not only inspires but prepares young women with the skills and mentality necessary to succeed.

With boldness, I approached 23 of Australia's most prominent female leaders to contribute 500 words each on lessons they have learned along the way and insights into their journey to success.

Most of us see the waves but not the undercurrent. What we see from aspirational leaders are very often their successes and achievements from the outside. Sometimes, what we fail to appreciate is the hard work, the courage, the determination and the many tough lessons that have carried them this far. What I hope to uncover in this book is precisely their journey and the lessons of how they got there, beyond and beneath the success everybody sees. These remarkable women wrote their stories not with their pens, but with their hearts – hearts that long to see the next generation of young women rise up to leadership positions and acquire that seat at the table. Every page of this book is filled with wisdom charged with immense power to see careers transformed, boundaries crushed, and most importantly dreams realised.

As much as I would like to embellish on the journey that I have embarked on, the realisation of this book was not actually that much of a bumpy ride. In fact, it was so smooth that it took me by surprise. I was blown away by how well this idea was received, taken aback by the immense support that flooded my way and overwhelmed by the generosity of the amazing businesswomen who shared their wisdom so unreservedly.

By the time I first put all the manuscripts together and read each word in this book, tears were streaming down my face. I was truly moved, not only because a dream that had seemed so unrealistic for me at the time of its inception had actually been brought to life, but also because I was so convinced that this book will most definitely lead to many more dreams being fulfilled.

It has been a truly humbling journey. I am just amazed to see how far sheer boldness has taken me – boldness to see and believe in possibilities rather than limitations. It was the inability to conform, and enough self-belief to challenge the boundaries others placed on me, that have always delivered for me in the end. Considering that I barely passed my Year 10 English exam, the task of publishing a book seemed far beyond my reach, not to mention being able to influence our corporate world alongside some of Australia's most powerful business women.

Looking back now to the time when I started Little Girl Big Dream, it was the beginning of a dream, one I thought would never take off, but in merely three years, not only has it gone from strength to strength, this dream has grown bigger and better with the completion of this book.

I hope you will enjoy reading this book as much as I have loved putting it together.

Let the journey begin.

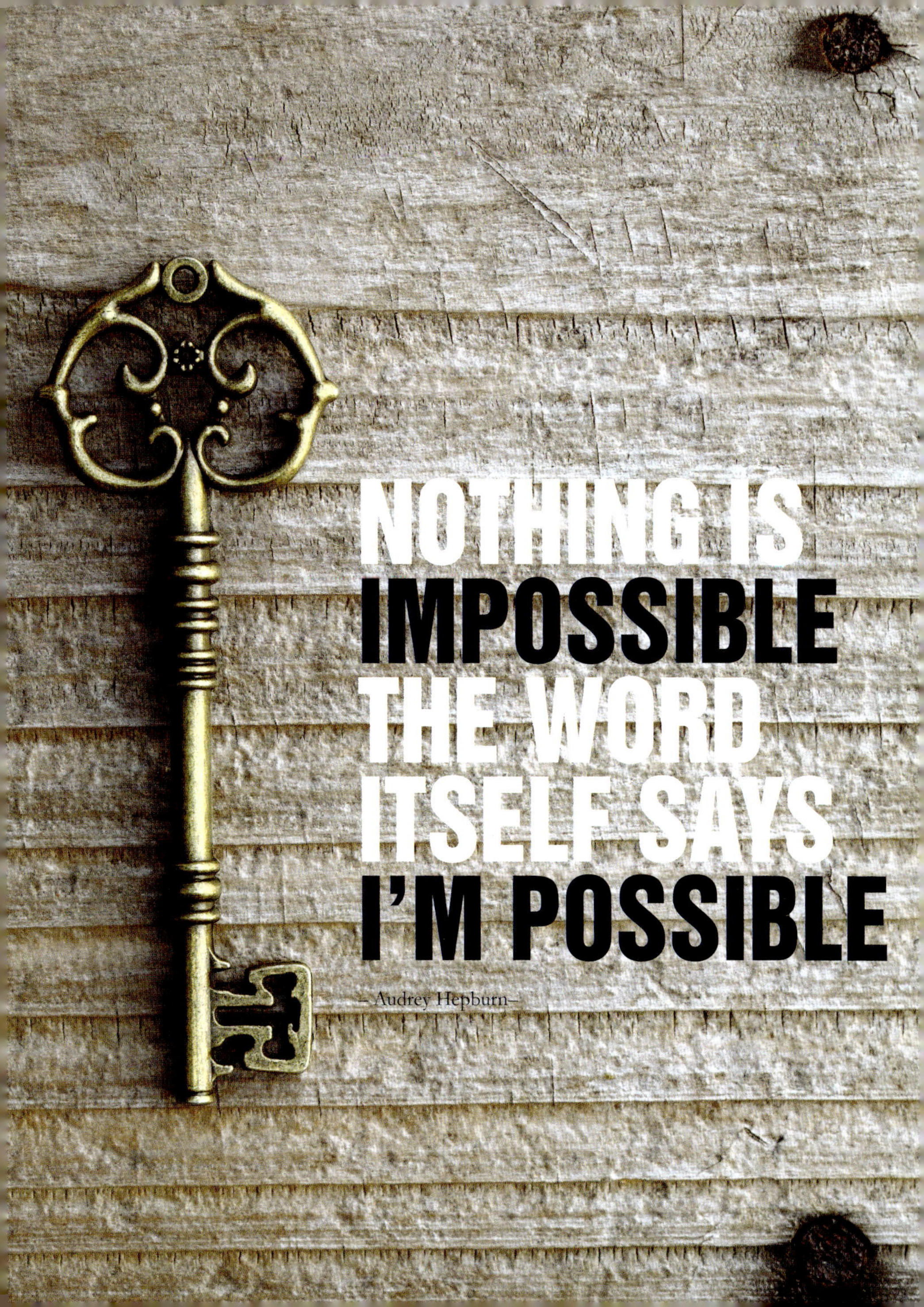
NOTHING IS
IMPOSSIBLE
THE WORD
ITSELF SAYS
I'M POSSIBLE
– Audrey Hepburn–

Amy Smith

CEO, Rise Productions

Former CEO, Jenny Craig Australia and New Zealand

Once bit, twice determined

WE ARE BORN WITH TWO LIVES. The one we are born into and the one we choose. I am a strong supporter of the saying, "Don't live your life for the length of it, live it for the breadth of it as well". I never wanted my life or my career to be limited by someone else's limited view of me! It has taken time to feel good in my own skin and to know that I can achieve great things based on the experience of having done so, over and over, thus ruling out the possibility that it's a fluke! Time and timing are important. I now value time rather than get frustrated by it. I have learnt that time isn't always just about years; it is about experiencing and feeling the life we have fully and feeling profoundly grateful for the simple fact that we breathe, as much as for the things we have and do on a daily basis.

Life is about choices and not all of them can be great, but being aware and present in life is important so you don't miss anything and can see things from a different vantage point when you need to get a different perspective. I have tried to be open minded and keep my eyes and heart open and in the main, this has served me well for even when I have been betrayed, I have learnt valuable lessons too. I believe boundaries are merely conventions and are able to be broken if you can conceive of how. That's why I value courage and creativity in both business and in people as if you have these qualities you will always be able to overcome the handbrakes life sometimes serves up and find a way to grow and flourish.

Power is an interesting thing. When you have it the whole world calls you and when you don't you find out who really cares for you. I believe power comes not from hate but from truth – both being true to one's self and seeing the truth – and this takes courage. So much of what limits us is an illusion and we lose touch with our inner voice and get distracted from our core purpose. I love transformation and building businesses that are open hearted, open minded and can fulfill a meaningful role in our lives. I am not simply a change agent who comes in and upsets the apple cart and leaves. I have learnt to be a good builder and know that with great vision and plenty of tenacity, it is possible to build something that has long lasting success.

If I could change one thing it would be that I had spent more time focusing on my true purpose rather than trying to be what others expected. For a long time I struggled and strained so hard to be different, instead of listening to my inner voice and going with my flow. Finding your flow is important, because you cannot achieve anything if all you are doing is forcing yourself into shapes that don't fit you. Living fully and flourishing means knowing your purpose and finding the right fit. No matter how good it is, you will always need to find the energy to thrive in the face of adversity but it is a lot easier when you are doing what you love.

Hence my motto 'Once bit, twice determined'. The point is not to avoid getting bitten in life, but what you do when it happens and hurts and how much you can learn and grow from the experience – both professionally and personally.

DON'T LIVE YOUR LIFE FOR THE LENGTH OF IT, LIVE IT FOR THE BREADTH OF IT AS WELL.

As a leader, my job is to create, energise, inspire, and motivate people to achieve a vision. The day I do not bring my energy and passion to work is the day I stop being effective. I have always said to those who I have worked with that if they are not feeling better off for having me around, then what is the point of my leadership? In other words, leadership is a skill, but it is also gift and I am grateful for the opportunity to lead businesses throughout my career because each day we have the wonderful opportunity to choose to celebrate the experiences right in front of us and if we get it right, to change someone's life for the better. And dreams don't come any better than that.

Carolyn Creswell

Founder & Managing Director,
Carman's Fine Foods
2012 Telstra Australian Business
Woman of the Year

The story of the Mexican fisherman...

A boat docked in a tiny Mexican village. An American tourist complimented the Mexican fisherman on the quality of his fish and asked how long it took him to catch them.

"Not very long," answered the Mexican.

"But then, why didn't you stay out longer and catch more?" asked the American.

The Mexican explained that his small catch was sufficient to meet his needs and those of his family.

The American asked, "But what do you do with the rest of your time?"

"I sleep late, fish a little, play with my children, and take a siesta with my wife. In the evenings, I go into the village to see my friends, have a few drinks, play the guitar, and sing a few songs... I have a full life."

The American interrupted, "I have an MBA from Harvard and I can help you!

"You should start by fishing longer every day. You can then sell the extra fish you catch. With the extra revenue, you can buy a bigger boat. With the extra money the larger boat will bring, you can buy a second one and a third one and so on until you have an entire fleet of trawlers.

"Instead of selling your fish to a middleman, you can negotiate directly with the processing plants and maybe even open your own plant. You can then leave this little village and move to Mexico City, Los Angeles, or even New York City!

From there you can direct your huge enterprise."

"How long would that take?" asked the Mexican.

"Twenty, perhaps twenty-five years," replied the American.

"And after that?"

"Afterwards? That's when it gets really interesting," answered the American, laughing. "When your business gets really big, you can start selling stocks and make millions!"

"Millions? Really? And after that?"

"After that you'll be able to retire, live in a tiny village near the coast, sleep late, play with your children, catch a few fish, take a siesta, and spend your evenings drinking and enjoying with your friends!"

I heard this story a few years ago and I love it for so many reasons. I believe the journey of our life is more important than what we think the destination will look like. What will our days look like? Our years? I think sometimes we are aiming for the faster, bigger and shinier, and that does not necessarily bring you happiness. Thinking about what you are going to do day in day out and finding meaning, purpose and passion in those days is more important than your pay packet. If you love what you do, like I do, it does not feel like work. It is a little like the saying if you watch your pennies the dollars will take care of themselves. If you plan your days, your life will take care of itself too. Be brave, be strong, follow your gut and be true to yourself. And if you see someone without a smile, give them yours.

A SHIP IN PORT IS SAFE
but
THAT'S NOT WHAT SHIPS
are
BUILT FOR
– Grace Murray Hopper –

Catriona Noble

CEO, McDonald's Australia

Always do what you truly believe in.

AS SOMEONE WHO – some might say – bucked the trend on my career path, I often have discussions with my wonderful 13-year-old daughter who is quite risk-averse. I try to encourage her to be less afraid of making mistakes, and she and I often laugh together about how I'm trying to get her into trouble, but that's not what's happening. I'm attempting to develop within her a confidence in her own opinions and beliefs. After all, any time you do something it's better than doing nothing.

HAVING A LACK OF CONFIDENCE TENDS TO LEAD TO A LACK OF ACTION.

This is an important consideration for women entering business because the real difference between men and women in the workplace, in my opinion, is that young men have great belief in their own opinion, while young women don't.

In order to have greater faith in your own opinions you mustn't be too afraid of failing, or of the consequences of being wrong. Men in the workplace are happier to be wrong, and that means they constantly learn valuable lessons about how to be right.

Of course we all have doubts about ourselves. But you can learn to look at the facts and come up with a decision and, most importantly, to be responsible for that decision. Ask yourself what's the worst that can happen. Usually it's not much. If you make the right decision and take action then you'll have learnt something and earned respect. If you were wrong and you took action, you'll possibly learn an even more valuable lesson. There is very little success without failure.

One of my biggest and most controversial decisions was to leave university, where I was studying Economics/Law, to work full-time at McDonald's, where I had worked part-time since I was fourteen years and nine months old. A lot of people doubted my decision, but I have a love of learning and I felt I was learning more and gaining more relevant skills at McDonald's, and at various courses on which the company was sending me, than I was at university.

I remember telling my father and I expected him to kick back a little, to disagree and try to talk me out of it. But he listened to my reasoning, agreed that I had weighed up all of the options and offered his full support. He had worked hard to develop within me a great self-belief. This decision was a result of that.

Since then I have had moments in my career when I knew I wasn't doing what my managers wanted me to do. In some cases I made some adjustments and toned things down a little. In some cases I did not. But I never crossed the line into doing something I didn't believe in. You must always be willing to moderate your behaviour but at the same time, you must always know where that line is. You gain this knowledge through experience, and if you always do what you truly believe in, then even if you shake things up a little you will end up having greater credibility.

Leaving university and believing in my ability to make good decisions certainly worked for me. There may have been small challenges along the way, but on the positive side it has offered me wonderful career success as well as the confidence to ensure life is as much about family as it is about work. And I hope that my own example will help to teach my daughter that risk as a result of self-belief isn't always such a terrible thing.

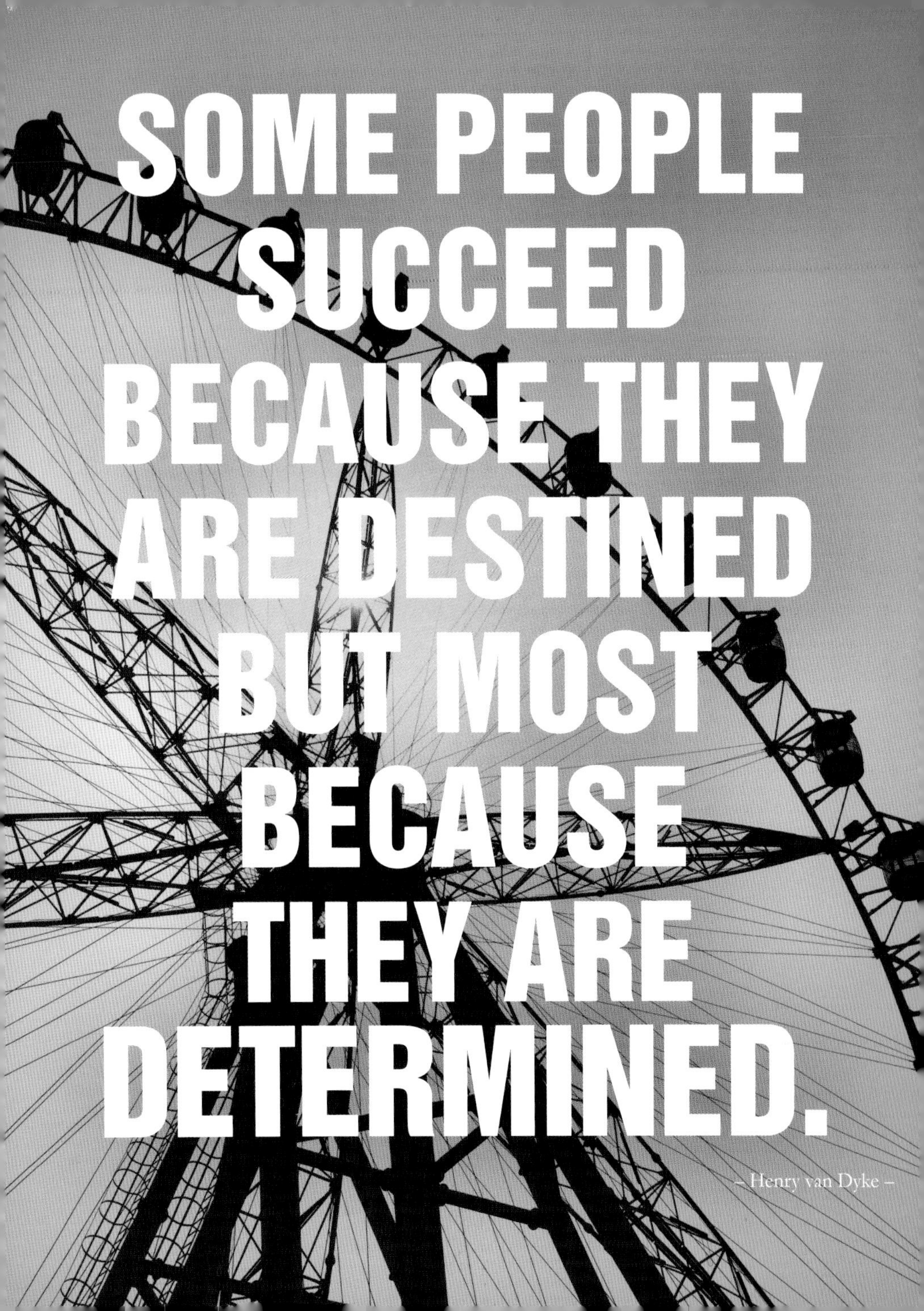
SOME PEOPLE SUCCEED BECAUSE THEY ARE DESTINED BUT MOST BECAUSE THEY ARE DETERMINED.
– Henry van Dyke –

Catriona Watson-Lamb

General Manager Global Marketing and Communications, Bendon Group

OH IF ONLY I could borrow Michael J Fox's time machine from *Back to the Future* and meet myself twenty years ago – back in the day when I had cheekbones and hipbones that stuck out and my week's salary would get blown on Friday night's outfit! I would sit down with that younger me, buy her a coffee and pass on these words of experience I have learnt (sometimes the hard way) during my career:

BE YOUR AUTHENTIC SELF

How tiring is it to try and act like someone other than yourself from 9am to 6pm five days a week? How much harder is it to build strong relationships across an organisation when you have to spend conscious energy remembering your work persona?

You will find in fact people will be more engaged, enjoy your company more, feel more motivated by your leadership when you show them consistently the real you and you in turn will immensely enjoy being at work so much more when you can show sides of yourself that you previously hid away.

MAKE TIME TO THINK

Days, weeks, months and even years can literally become lost trapped on a mouse wheel of endless emails, meetings and company processes where your development and opportunities to really grow are starved by the lack of time to really think and stretch your mind.

You have to take control of your time, to treat it like a precious commodity and use it to get the best out of yourself and your performance. Put time for yourself to think first (not last) and schedule it in daily with a discipline to keep it and use it well.

TAKE ACCOUNTABILITY

It's so much easier to just whinge away to colleagues, to family, to blame your manager, the company culture, the role you have. It is however your choice not to do anything but complain or worry or stress yourself and others. And it can also be your choice to identify what the issues are, why they are occurring, what are some potential solutions and who is best to engage with.

YOU CAN HAVE IT ALL JUST WORK OUT WHAT THIS MEANS TO YOU

Stop looking at other women's career choices as the litmus test on what you should be doing with yours. There is not one other person in the world with your exact circumstances and who knows what you want to do with your life. Discuss your dreams and plans with your key supporters and those who need to help you make it happen, try it and if for some reason it doesn't work out, try something different.

IT'S A JOB

Give every role, every opportunity 100 per cent of your passion and know-how but stop short of giving it every part of your mind and heart. As Marilyn Monroe once said "A career is wonderful but you can't curl up with it on a cold night."

Take control of your time,
to treat it like a precious
commodity and use it to get
the best out of yourself.

Gillian Franklin

Founder and Managing Director, The Heat Group

Be in love with your life. Every minute of it.

– Jack Kerouac –

I have been fortunate to have a successful life so far. However those who know me also know that it has been peppered with many hurdles and painful experiences. My key philosophy has always been to use every experience, whether good or bad, as a character building opportunity, and to focus on using these experiences to make me a better person. One example of turning a negative life experience into a positive was my cancer diagnosis in 2008. While I know that the experience is different for everyone, for me it was very important that instead of letting it get me down, I made a pact with myself that I would focus on all the good things about having cancer. Strange concept perhaps, but the list wasn't actually that hard to put together. I saved a significant amount of money on hairdressers and leg waxing appointments because for six months I didn't have any hair! I could get ready very quickly in the morning because all I had to do with my hair was throw on a wig. I reflected on the love and care of my friends and family and this in turn reinforced my love of life. I also used my cancer to raise awareness and funds for the Breast Cancer Network so there was a positive outcome for the community.

It is amazing how powerful your mind is if you apply yourself – you can deal with any circumstances how YOU want to. Cancer also brought something very important to my attention – that there was absolutely nothing I would like to change about my life. Many people who are diagnosed decide to change the way they live – some decide to work less, spend more time with family, travel, etc. – but I realised that there was absolutely nothing I would change. I was very happy. This was something great to focus on as well.

IF YOU DON'T RUN YO OWN LIFE SOMEBOD

Of course, you don't need to wait for a cancer diagnosis to ask yourself, "Am I happy with my life?" I would encourage anyone to reflect and ask themselves, "If I only had one more year to live, what would I change?" And strive to change those things until your answer is "absolutely nothing". I should add that in my case I work incredibly, incredibly hard, many would say too hard! However this is exactly how I want it – I love working and would not change it for the world.

The second point I'd like to make is to stress the importance of knowing what you want, and planning for it. So if, for example, you are twenty, conceptualise your life when you will be thirty. Do you picture yourself as married, have children, work full time or part time, travel, work long hours and have a career, or have a less demanding role and spend time training for a marathon? The choices you make about your education and career need to be planned in the context of your WHOLE life, not just your career goals. In my case, I wanted to be a General Manager before I was thirty. This was not about being a GM, but about having the flexibility and income to be able to have children and keep working, so I needed to be able to afford a nanny and that meant I needed to have a senior role. Women often feel almost obliged to make choices that end up as a compromise for them – this is not right or necessary. I want to say this to you: don't allow anyone to influence you to compromise on your dreams. You can do anything you want if you know what that is and put plans in place to get there.

UR

ELSE WILL.

– John Atkinson –

Ghazaleh Lyari

Founder and Managing Director,
Ghermez Cupcakes

WHAT I HAVE LEARNT ON MY JOURNEY...

THERE IS NO SUBSTITUTE FOR HARD WORK AND EXPERIENCE

There are no shortcuts in life. Don't look for the easy way. Regardless of the outcome, the experience of the journey itself will change you into a better, richer, and more refined person.

WHO YOU KNOW WILL COME FROM WHAT YOU KNOW

'Who you know' will be instrumental to your success in life, but 'what you do' and 'what you know' will drive who you know. 'Earn' your contacts by working hard and helping others along the way. Be generous with your time and insights to others who appreciate it. The more you give, the more you will receive.

EARN YOUR MENTORS

You will attract your mentors by demonstrating what you are made of. Don't approach strangers to be your mentors. That special relationship grows when someone you respect recognises your special brand of keen interest and capabilities, and thinks he/she can help you go forward faster. Create opportunities to be around those you respect, and work towards being 'chosen' as a mentee.

THE HARDER YOU WORK THE MORE LUCK YOU WILL HAVE

If there is such a thing as luck, you will only experience it by participating in the game, by trying hard, and not giving up at the first sign of disappointment. Luck doesn't knock on the door of passive observers. As Wayne Gretzky said, "You miss 100 per cent of the shots you don't take".

NOTHING WILL STAY THE SAME

Nothing in life will stay the same. Anticipate and embrace change in every aspect of your life. It will always offer the opportunity to begin a new chapter in life.

BE GRATEFUL TO THOSE WHO HELP YOU

One of the most precious lessons my parents ever taught me was that "No one owes me anything". Consider yourself lucky when someone takes an interest in helping you. Get into the habit of writing thank you notes. Never take for granted what others do for you.

EXPECT TO LIVE THROUGH MULTIPLE CHAPTERS IN LIFE

Stay open to opportunities to experience various jobs, live in different cities, and embrace different adventures. If you are lucky enough you will live multiple different chapters in your life, each taking you on an enchanted journey and enriching a different aspect of your personality.

LIFE WITHOUT FRIENDSHIPS IS A LIFE HALF-LIVED

Invest time and energy in a handful of good friendships. True friends will be your compass in life and help you stay on your path.

WHEN THE GOING GETS TOUGH...

Think of what matters to you most in life, to keep things in perspective. Business ventures, jobs, and opportunities will come and go. Keep grounded by staying connected to those you love. They will remind you that tough times will always pass.

GHAZALEH LYARI

NEVER LET SUCCESS
GET TO YOUR HEAD.
NEVER LET FAILURE
GET TO YOUR heart.
– Unknown –

Jacinta Tynan

News Presenter, Journalist, Author, Mum and
Patron of SISTER2Sister

Image courtesy of Sunday Life

Oh, the lessons I have learnt along the way of my life and career. If only I knew then what I know now...

HAVE REGRETS

It's easy to say not to have regrets but we just will. And that's not a bad thing. There's nothing wrong with regrets if we add them to our arsenal of what not to do the next time similar circumstances arise. The trick is to not allow them to hold us back from creating the life we want, forever admonishing ourselves for paths we wish we had or hadn't taken.

I once knocked back a phenomenal job opportunity (one I could only dream of now) because I didn't want to let down my then employer. I was also worried that – despite encouragement from people who believed in me – I may not be up for the job. I feared I might be out of my league. What if I fell flat on my face and ended up worse off? After I declined the offer, the employer who I had felt such loyalty for, sidelined me so I "wouldn't get too big for my boots". I learned pretty swiftly (and harshly) that loyalty is just as much about loyalty to ourselves as anyone else.

I no longer regret that decision (although I beat myself up about it for a while) because, by not taking that job, I set myself on a path that in hindsight I realise was necessary for my growth – personally and professionally. There's no doubt it would have been a wonderful opportunity but I would never have learnt as much or taken steps to seek out my own fulfillment, had I slipped into success so early.

FIND A MENTOR

I didn't. I would have loved to have a mentor but I didn't know where to find one. I have no doubt my path would have been a little smoother and less confusing if I had had a trusted and consistent person to talk to for life, love and career advice. That is why I am such a big believer in mentoring, and give my support to the SISTER2Sister mentor program for disadvantaged teenage girls.

It also helps if we be the person we want to have in our life: self loving, reliable, consistent, kind, positive. Hold yourself... especially if there is no one else to do it.

DO THERAPY

Or self improvement of some sort. We can always strive to be a better person and to understand ourselves more – why we act and react the way we do. I used to think self analysis was a short term thing to do until we are "fixed". I now know I will keep at it always. Contentment is a lifelong goal.

BE CONSCIOUS

I wish I had known earlier that what we focus on – what we think and talk about – is what we attract more of. It is liberating to take responsibility rather than blame other people or circumstances for what transpires.

LEARNT TO MEDITATE

The quickest way to find consciousness. Since I learnt to meditate (twenty minutes twice a day) I have become far more mindful of what I think and say. And far more chilled.

VALUE FRIENDSHIPS

Surround ourselves with people who get us and want the best for us instead of yapping at the heels of those who want us to change. If the central aim is to fit in, we never will.

THERE IS NO DEADLINE

There is no time limit on our dreams. Who drew the line in the sand that said you have to be on track by a certain age or it's too late? If we are authentic with ourselves and have courage it's never too late to work out what we want to do and be, and follow that up.

I am only just accepting that we are exactly where we are meant to be. Right now is the perfect time to make changes and create the life we were "meant" to have. No matter how old we are or what "mistakes" we have made along the way.

BIG
THINGS
often
have
small
beginnings
– Unknown –

Jackie Frank

Publisher/Editor, *marie claire*

NEVER A PROBLEM, ALWAYS AN OPPORTUNITY

LESSON #1:

Live your life with passion. We all love people who are passionate, and if you find a job that inspires you and work hard at it, you will make it.

I never planned for this kind of career; my passion was to be a beauty therapist. After leaving school, I soon found a job at a Melbourne salon. I was living the dream, which then came crashing down when I was involved in a car accident. The doctors told me the injuries I suffered to my back meant I couldn't continue with the physical demands of this work. I was devastated, and I didn't know what to do. Then my mother heard about a family friend who covered the social pages of *Harper's Bazaar* in Melbourne – she needed some help. I jumped at the chance. While working there being a beauty therapist part-time, I noticed that a lot of Melbourne fashion brands weren't being featured in the magazine, so I asked if I could send clothes to the main office in Sydney. I wasn't thinking, "I'm not a fashion editor. I shouldn't be doing this." I just thought, "What else can I do to help?" Before long, the pages of the magazine were filling up with my stock. Then a job came up in the Sydney office, and they offered it to me. I didn't even ask about the title or the money. I was so keen to work in this industry that I would have done it for free.

It will happen for you if you stay true to who you are

LESSON #2:

Keep your mind open to opportunities. Work really hard so that when your chance comes along, you are ready to seize it.

Fast-forward a few years and I was working on *Mademoiselle* magazine in New York City. A new editor came onboard, brought in her own team and fired everyone else. My working visa was attached to my job, so I needed to take action fast. I heard that *Mademoiselle*'s new fashion director was from *marie claire* UK, so I called them. They offered me a job based in New York, which then introduced me to the amazing world of *marie claire.* Some people said I was lucky, but I believe hard work makes for good luck.

LESSON #3:

Don't be who other people want you to be. Always stay true to yourself. You have to believe in your talents – this is the real secret to success.

My mum says, "It will happen for you if you stay true to who you are." I know firsthand that sometimes being yourself doesn't seem like the right option, but I've always tried to live by Mum's words. I remember as a teenager, when I was trying to fit in, I read the book *What It Is To Be Normal.* Afterwards, I worked out that being "normal" just means being average. Who wants to be average? I decided then to just be me.

Jackie

FIND A JOB
YOU ARE
PASSIONATE
ABOUT AND
WORK HARD
AT IT.
YOU WILL
MAKE IT.

Jane Huxley

Managing Director, Pandora Australia and New Zealand

THE ONLY WAY TO DO GREAT WORK,

is to love what you do. – Steve Jobs –

WORK HARD, love what you do and have the courage to say what you really think. We've all heard those words before, but now nearly 25 years or so into my career for me they have never been truer. In a career which has really been all about learning (and therefore never gets tired) the best lesson I can pass on is how to not take things personally. I was once going through some issues in the office, where I felt the work I was doing was under attack, making poor decisions, not performing to expectations and that I was letting others down. Have you ever felt like that? It's exhausting. Of course, most of this was imagined, but nevertheless, that was my reality. I was talking this through with an incredible mentor of mine who quickly realized that I was taking everything personally. This is what she taught me. "Jane," she said, "when you are driving to your office take a look up at the sign on the top of the building. The day that it says HUXLEY is the day that it's personal. Every other day when it says *<insert your company name here>*, then it's business." The next day, I started looking up at that sign, and you know what… it never said Huxley. It was never personal.

Sometimes though, it takes practice to make a lesson come to life. For a long time after that, at the top of each page of the book I would use to take notes in, I would write the letters INP. To me, this meant it's not personal. Through a combination of remembering her words, looking up at that building, and the visual reminder, I learned how to reframe my thinking around the business first. It was a valuable lesson about context and it helped me to become more effective in my contributions. And it saved a lot of tears too.

DON'T S
SUR
YOUR CO
– Unknown –

INK YOUR DREAMS.

R-SIZE

RAGE AND ABILITIES.

When I look back on it now, this particular lesson gave me insight into what I believe are two of the core characteristics of successful leaders – self-awareness and self-management.

The principal of self-awareness is your ability to step outside of yourself, your work, or your behaviours, to assess them honestly; using a lens of how you think others might view you. Self-management is complementary to this, and is the ability to act on what you believe are your greatest challenges or opportunities to develop. This may include observing behaviours you need to model, working with a selection of mentors, or reflecting on the values that you hold and whether or not they "fit" with the work you are doing. Increasingly smart organisations are looking for not only what you can do, but also how you go about doing it. Eventually I believe that behaviors will be more important than skills. And I believe that women will shine.

There is an empowering kind of courage that comes with getting these attributes in alignment. And it is this courage that will allow you to fail and learn, to build your networks, to stretch your thinking above and beyond. And ultimately, to love what you do.

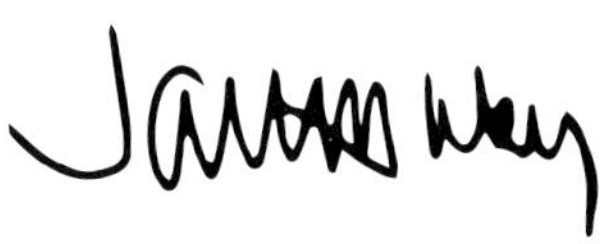

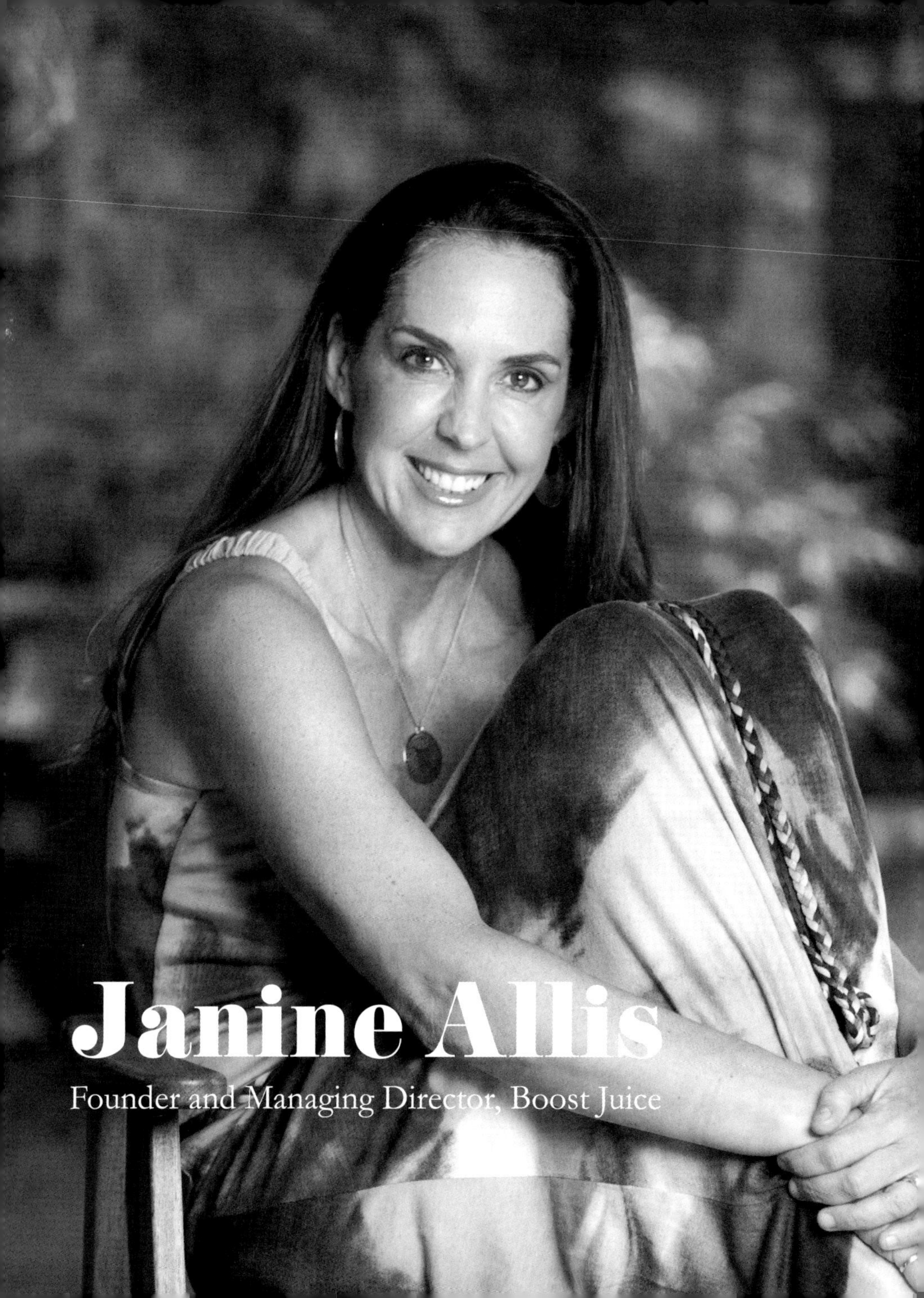

Janine Allis

Founder and Managing Director, Boost Juice

Life isnt about finding yourself. Life is about creating yourself.

– George Bernard Shaw –

I THINK OF the most amazing life I have had and the amazing life still to come and it would not have been that way if it were not for the good, bad and ugly of the past. So what words of wisdom would I give you as advice? That is a really hard question.

It is not that I do not want you to have fun, make mistakes and live, because that is exactly what you HAVE to do; I just hope that any mistakes that you do end up making be only memories and lessons of the past and that they do not affect the rest of your life. It is about the choices you make, and if you make more good choices than bad and if luck is on your side most of the time, then you get to have a look back at your past and smile, shiver and laugh at the foolishness of growing up and the fun and freedom that you have on the journey called LIFE.

The secret to being young is to have fun and live a free life, make mistakes and discover the world around you; and work out how you fit into this world. I have made too many mistakes in my life to count, and I would not change one of them, because they have made me who and what I am today, and to be honest, I actually quite like who I have become. I am certainly still faulty, but happy that I am working through all of those faults.

You are going to make mistakes; that is one thing that is guaranteed, but you have to make sure that the mistakes cannot hurt you or anyone else. My wish for you is that you make wise choices, cross that scary line every now and then and always see the best in everyone.

Choose great people, who make you feel good about yourself. Don't let anyone treat you poorly and always treat people how you would love to be treated. It is not okay for people to undermine you and treat you without the respect you deserve. One thing my husband told me that I will always remember; people treat you how you let them.

Jump out of a plane, learn to scuba dive, plan a trip around the world. Don't be afraid to embrace life and take some risks. Don't take the easy way out, because enjoying the fruit of your hard earned success is that much sweeter. Dream big dreams and aim for the most unimaginable, all because you can! But most importantly, know that there is nothing you cannot do or have in your life. It is yours for the taking. Just believe it, say it and then make it happen.

What a wonderful anticipation of the great journey ahead of you. Enjoy the euphoria of being young, free, passionate, ambitious and alive. And make good choices.

DON'T BE
AFRAID TO
EMBRACE LIFE
AND TAKE
SOME RISKS.

IF YOU DON'T
CHASE YOUR
DREAMS
YOU WILL NEVER
CATCH THEM.

WHAT'S YOUR BIG DREAM?
#LGBD #BIGDREAMS

Janine Garner

Founder and Director, Little Black Dress Group

HERE ARE 8 TIPS

for making success happen with, if not ease, then some grace and perhaps a bit less stress!

1. SUCCESS IS A MINDSET.

Never forget this. Throughout the years you will experience the good, the bad and the downright ugly in terms of business and what you can expect from those involved in it; but through it all key factors will be self belief, a positive attitude, seeing the opportunity to learn, and having a mindset for success.

2. BE COURAGEOUS IN EVERYTHING YOU DO.

Have the courage to stand in your own spotlight; to use your voice, to ask for help and to be vulnerable. Don't be afraid to be different, and to challenge the status quo – because it is through the challenge that change happens.

3. UNDERSTAND WHAT MAKES UP YOUR VALUE SYSTEM AND OWN IT. LIVE IT. WORK IT.

Your value system is unique to you and it is your responsibility to take ownership of it. There are times when it will be challenged or when you will give in to others' values – and you will look back and kick yourself, and wish you had trusted your intuition. Don't ever mistrust that intuition and that gut feeling. It is a key part of you, and you should learn that it is one of your best assets. Ignore it at your peril.

4. BE PERSISTENT THROUGH THE GOOD AND THE BAD.

Persistence will be the extra oomph when others may crumble. Wasn't it Thomas Edison who said 'genius is ninety nine percent perspiration, one per cent inspiration'? He was right. It is hard work that gets you where you want to go. Inspiration and dreams are absolutely essential to making your story happen – but unless you are prepared to dedicate yourself to that story, it will never jump off the page and into real life.

5. FIND YOUR TRIBE.

Don't try to fit in with others simply because you think you should. You are the average of the five people, with whom you surround yourself most closely. So make the most of those people. Find like-minded thinkers, believers and dreamers. Work together. Collaborate. Support each other. Make the journey fun as well as hard work. It will be so much more enjoyable and far more possible.

6. LOOK AFTER YOURSELF!

You will forget this at times, I know, especially in the early stages, when you are trying to get things up and running. True success is a reflection of total vitality. Allow yourself the time to celebrate every little stage and each small achievement; to dream, to create, to rest and above all to think.

7. VIEW LEARNING AND STUDY AS AN INVESTMENT.

Learn continuously. Keep your eyes and ears open to everything around you. Recognise the gifts that are presented to you – to us – every day. See the value in the people you meet. Question them. Question their wealth of knowledge. Take in every available resource. Never ever lose sight of your goals – to know as much as you can about your business, your industry, your world.

8. ABOVE ALL ELSE – PLAN.

When you have made a plan, make another plan. And then have a contingency plan. Above all – be prepared to make those plans fluid. Five-year plans are fantastic. But they cannot be rigid. You will find that your life, in business and in general, will change at a quick fire pace. You need to be prepared for this. Planning in advance can be advantageous, but you need to be able to flow and change according to circumstances, and be willing to adapt to different circumstances.

Enjoy the ride!

ACTION IS THE FUNDAMENTAL KEY TO ALL SUCCESS.

– Pablo Picasso –

Jayne Hrdlicka

Group CEO, Jetstar

To accomplish great things...

YOU MUST NOT ONLY ACT – BUT ALSO *dream*
YOU MUST NOT ONLY PLAN – BUT ALSO *believe*

CONGRATULATIONS! You were born into a lifetime of extraordinary opportunities as a girl with ambition. My advice to you is simple. Dream big dreams and go for it! Always set your sights high and see the possible. And never, ever, let anyone tell you that you are not amazing or that you cannot achieve your goals.

It all starts with believing deeply that you can do or be anything that you want to be. That yours is the world of possibilities and that you can make it what you will. You will need to work hard, keep your eyes and ears open to what is required to succeed, and learn how to deliver. You will need to be courageous at times and sometimes take uncomfortable risks. You will have moments of self-doubt – but you keep that to yourself or your trusted few!

You will have both men and women who try to deflate your ambition. People who will tell you subtly and sometimes directly that you cannot have it all, that it is a man's world and that you are not good enough. Don't let them get under your skin. Instead, listen carefully to the feedback you get, and act on it. This will almost surely require you to modify your style as you become more senior. Put your hand up for coaching, and personal and professional development opportunities, and be the one always looking for feedback to improve.

Invest in building infrastructure around you when you have children. There are lots of things that need doing to maintain your home and to support your growing family. Don't try to do all of that yourself, plus be a great mum, plus advance your career. Something has to give, so find a way through family, friends and outside help to create a model that works for you and helps shoulder the mix of responsibilities you need to manage. It is achievable, but only if you have a plan and don't try to do it all yourself.

Also, ask advice from other women who have managed work and career; they are a fountain of wisdom and perspective. Be clear about your priorities and manage all the trade-offs in life accordingly.

The last thought I would leave with you is to think about your career as a journey. You can never be sure exactly where you will end up but you want to be in a position where every new career step you take has the potential to open up new opportunities in the future.

Investing in relationships along the way is a vital part of the journey, and seeking roles with people who you admire and respect will never be a bad move. Always think about the building blocks you are laying down, both in relationships and networks, as well as the substance of your job experiences. Actively engage in 'taking stock' and making sure you are headed in the right direction.

Good luck to you – your life is yours to make.

WHEN EVERYTHING SEEMS TO BE GOING AGAINST YOU, REMEMBER THAT AN AIRPLANE TAKES OFF AGAINST THE WIND, NOT WITH IT.

– Henry Ford –

Kim Lion
Managing Director,
Universal McCann Melbourne

Use your smile to change the world.
Dont let this world change your smile.

– Unknown –

MY MOTHER DIDN'T KNOW she was having identical twins until the moment I was born, when my sister was eagerly chasing my arrival (as announced by the delivering doctor). The year – 1970, and the era – second-wave feminism. Not only was I born into a time of championing women's cultural equality but, more potently, I was born with a constant companion, who would be the person with whom I would enter a lifetime of healthy competition.

Two little girls, smallest in every class, but constantly aware of how we ranked. Not compared with everyone else, but against each other. In sport, one would win the cross country, the other would come second. In school representation, one would be captain, the other prefect. We don't remember our other competition, only how each other had done. A heady mix of care and contest.

This omnipresent rivalry (albeit healthy) and the decade into which I was born (protesting to the world "you are woman, roar away!"), took its time dripping into my psyche. The takeout: both my twin and the era of my early education had relentlessly paired and scored me against one particular female and a whole generation of men, and boy am I glad that it did.

So now, 43 years later, what did that impact? I'm wonderfully content, restlessly ambitious and extremely happy. Though I don't fit the "happy" mould; I am unmarried (yet have a long and cherished partner, and circle of friends and family that love each other fully); childless (by choice, alongside a bounty of beautiful kids – nephew, cousins' and dear friends' offspring); and a fairly fractured sense of home (having lived in five cities and four countries in the last decade alone). I work in media and LOVE it. I am outnumbered by men at a senior level, however I don't call it out or wonder why more women aren't there. Instead, my colleagues are a group of professionals who take a lot of pride in what we do. We've all had similar history to one another; again ignoring gender, we believe in what we do and we like to be great at it.

To you, kindly reading this (man or woman) here's my main thought: don't get too attached to gender comparison. Instead, become a specialist observer of brilliance. There are certain behaviours I live by that I've picked up from careful observation of brilliant people:

1) BE CALM.

Commence by removing emotion when making a decision, and then reintroduce it (we are, after-all, human). Oscillate those thoughts and you'll be a caring and effective manager. My favourite saying: be hard on the issue, kind on the person.

2) COMPETITION IS HEALTHY...

and "the game" should be played in great spirit to you and the person or situation you are in. Respecting those around you by appreciating their perspective couldn't be more useful.

3) BE DRIVEN...

by how great you can be, know what you want and say so, make your calls about business not feelings, and be obsessed with what you can deliver.

4) DON'T BE TOO SERIOUS...

all the time.

Those are my four. You'll find your own. Do this by watching those around you, particularly those who are successful and happy. If there is someone who is awesome, follow them closely. Man or woman, they will be conscious of beating their competition, but at the same time generous, considered, and usually very much in charge of themselves.

And with that, I wish you extremely well and hope to meet you some day.

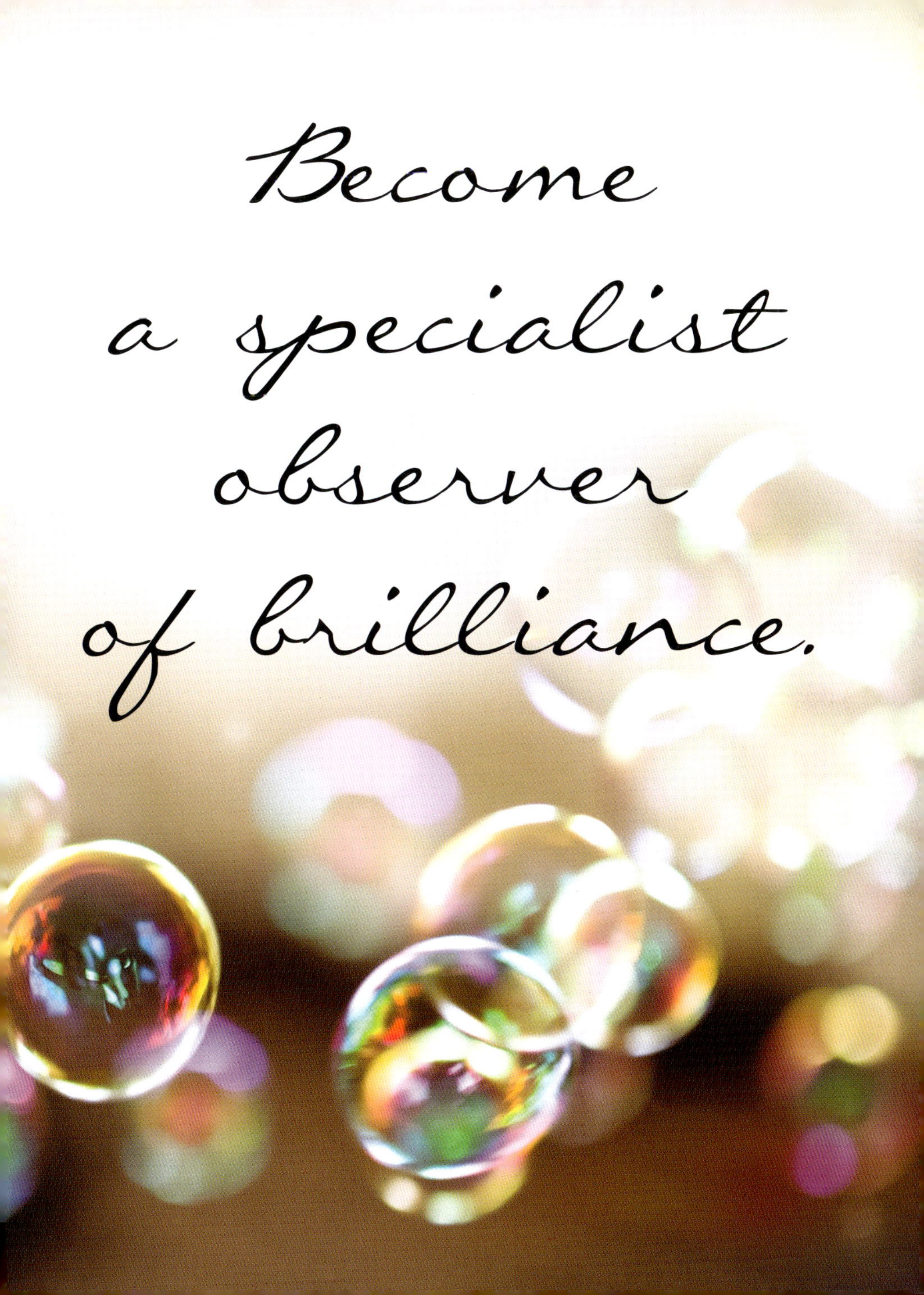
Become
a specialist
observer
of brilliance.

Kristina Karlsson

Founder and Creative Director, kikki K

Image courtesy of kikki K

I THINK DREAMING is the first step to actually achieving. I've always loved the quote, 'Nothing happens unless first we dream.'

Some things might be achievable straight away, others might take a little while to get to, but I think it's so important to dream without limitations. You never know what you might achieve if you set your mind to it. This is something I constantly live by, and something I hope to inspire in other people – perhaps you, reading this book.

My initial career dream can be summarised in the '3am List' my partner, Paul, encouraged me to write as I restlessly questioned what it was that I wanted to do with my life. I wanted to start my own business, do something that connected me back to Sweden, do something with design, and something I would always love driving to work for on a Monday morning. This list gave me focus and, soon after, the idea for kikki.K was born. It came to me when I tried to set up a home office and struggled to find the gorgeous stationery products I was used to at home in Sweden.

If you're still searching for your passion, I encourage you to spend time working it out. Write down in your notebook what you are passionate about, what you love, what you don't like, what you would do if money were no object. I think most of us know what we love, it's just sometimes hard to work out the bridge between what you love and your skills. But if you are passionate about what you do, I really believe you can achieve anything if you truly want it.

believe in

of your o

– Eleanor Roosevelt –

the beauty in dreams.

By no means has my career journey been smooth-sailing. There have been so many challenges to deal with and so many new experiences from day one. I had no prior business knowledge, and English was my second language – and that was just the start. One of my key learnings, though, has been to be excited about change and excited about challenges. Together with a supportive team around you and guidance from wonderful, like-minded mentors, be open to welcome and foster change, learn from mistakes and focus on your vision, no matter how big the hurdles may be.

I had – and still have – a crystal-clear vision, and an enormous amount of passion for my dream and believe this is so, so important for anyone who wants to succeed with their career, or simply make the most of their life.

Larke Riemer

Director Women's Markets, Westpac

BE BOLD & BE CONFIDENT

FOR MORE THAN 20 years I've worked with Westpac, building and developing its programs to support women's personal and business wealth creation. It's taught me a lot about myself, and what women want in their life and career.

We want to learn from one another in a supportive environment. We want easy access to education, information, networking and finance opportunities. We want to be treated equally and with R.E.S.P.E.C.T.

I believe in equality and a diverse workplace, and if being treated with respect makes me a feminist, then I am proud to be a feminist.

No matter what we want at home or at work, if we are to succeed it is vital that we invest in relationships, that we connect and communicate effectively with others. Having mentors and sponsors – as well as taking on that role ourselves when we are able – is vital. It has provided me with lasting personal and career benefits. I would encourage you, whenever you uncover these little pots of gold – and they will come in all forms – grasp the opportunity and learn from each other.
A lot of the women I meet, especially those starting out, believe that if they haven't done it all by the time they reach their 20s or perhaps their early 30s, then they've failed.

I am here to tell you, it's not true.

New opportunities and the change they bring, provide us with new experiences and the chance to grow. They often lead us to rethink and even reassess our goals, which is why it's important to have flexibility in our lives to grow organically. Believing everything has to be done right here, right now puts unnecessary stress on us as people.

My advice is to stop and take the time to 'smell the roses'. We are different people in our 20s, 30s, 40s, 50s and 60s and our choices over time will have different outcomes. I married, had a family young, and have also spent had a long time in the workforce. This combination of family and work, has provided me with a bucket load of experience from which to draw.

One of the things I've learned is the need to be bold – to exert your influence at home, at work and in the community in a way that best suits who you are. Some of us shout from the rooftops. Others work more quietly. Your method is yours. The important thing to remember is to put your name forward. Research has shown us that women tend to go for a new or more senior position only if they're sure they can do 100 per cent of the job.

My question is: why move if you're not going to learn?

My rule of thumb is, be confident, understand what you are getting into and be prepared to learn on the job, and from the job. I always knew I was capable of 60 per cent of any new role for which I went. The rest was there for me to stretch myself through and learn from the experience.

A long time ago, Prince Charming swept me off my feet and it was wonderful, but things happen. Knowing you have remained in control of your own destiny, especially financially and economically, will be important for your wellbeing and your family's.

Having a career doesn't mean missing out on having a family. The important thing is to plan and look at what you and/or your partner need to do to make it work together, while realising the futures you deserve are your own responsibilities.

Planning together makes sense. In the end, however, a man is not a financial plan and no one will look after you better than you.

TAKE THE TIME TO
'SMELL THE ROSES'.

Layne Beachley

7-times World Surfing Champion
Founder and Director, Aim For The Stars

THE PAST OFFERS A RICH DATA BASE FROM WHICH WE CAN LEARN

IF YOU HAD the opportunity to go back in time and give your twenty year-old self some poignant words of advice, what would they be?

The one thing I would say to myself is "Lighten Up! Life is too short to take yourself seriously, so be kinder to yourself and those that you love".
I am my own world's worst critic, with high expectations, which I have constantly projected onto others. Fortunately I have had the guidance, love, support and patience of my friends and family to show me the 'light', so to speak, reminding me to focus on the important things and stop wasting my time worrying about everything out of my control.

We have all heard "only control the controllable." Honestly, if we go to the heart of this statement, the only thing we can actually control is the six inches between our ears. But where do you place your focus? Do you think about what you don't want? Or are you present enough to think about what you DO want?

Thought is expansive. What you think about, you create. The more you think about it, the faster you manifest it. Ultimately you are completely responsible for your current reality and the sooner you learn to accept accountability, the faster you will be able to create the life you truly want. As Dr John Demartini says, "The person that takes accountability and responsibility for their misconceptions and current perceptions becomes a leader."

Surfing has certainly taught me a lot about being in the present moment and going with the flow. The ocean is much more powerful than I am and, being a self confessed control freak on land, it has provided me some of the most wonderful life lessons. It demands me to surrender control, go with the flow and allow the ocean and Mother Nature to nurture and protect me. The minute I dive in the water cleanses my mind, body and soul.

But in other ways, I have noticed that the ocean tends to reflect my emotions. If I paddle out anxious, angry or frustrated I have a terrible time! I find myself being caught in the impact zone, falling off, missing waves and being constantly "slapped" in the head to snap out of it! This is when I have learned to giggle, which instantly dissolves the anger, bringing me back to the moment and putting everything back into perspective.

The immediate impact of choosing to put a smile on your face is very powerful. Now the fun truly begins. I am now relaxed, energised and free to enjoy the delight and freedom of expression that being in the ocean allows and encourages.

What do you do that enables you to reconnect with your true self?
How do you maintain perspective?
Do you take the time to make yourself happy, on a daily basis? Do you even know what makes you happy?
The quality of the questions you ask determines the quality of your life and your success.

Until you value you or invest in you, don't expect anyone else to.

Layne Beachley

If you really want to do something, you'll
FIND A WAY.
If you dont, you will find an excuse.

SHARE YOUR FAVOURITE QUOTE
#LGBD #INSPIRINGQUOTES

I'M NOT TELLING YOU IT'S GONNA BE EASY, I'M TELLING YOU IT'S GOING TO BE WORTH IT.

– Art Williams –

Lisa Messenger

Editor-in-Chief, *Renegade Collective*
CEO, The Messenger Group

SHOULD COULD WOULD DID.

I'VE BEEN ASKED to write words of encouragement, inspiration and advice for emerging young female leaders and entrepreneurs. But what I want to say applies equally to young men.

In a way I've been an entrepreneur my whole life but have been running my own company for nearly 12 years. My gender has never been an issue in business dealings; their successes or failures. I have been judged by both men and women solely on merit and have never been discriminated against because of my gender. I can say that hand on heart.

Never having worked in the corporate world I can't comment on whether it's harder to break the glass ceiling as a woman, and I do hear stories to that effect but, in my experience, opportunity and achievement boil down to great ideas, the willingness to put yourself on the line to realise them, backing yourself by believing you can do it and working your butt off.

I'm disturbed when I hear women in general being talked of as different species with diverse rules and values. You don't do things differently because you are a woman. It disturbs me even more when I hear women saying a failure was due to the fact they were female. Buying into the gender debate as a reason for this is an excuse and it's rubbish.

Nine years ago I wrote a book about happiness because I was so desperately unhappy at that juncture of my life. It became a bestseller, ironic when I did what was termed "veggie" English at school – the lowest of the low on the English food chain.

The success of "*Happiness Is …*" snowballed into seventeen more books that I wrote or co-authored, and 400-plus that my team and I published for clients. In March 2013, a year in the making, I fulfilled my biggest dream to date by launching *The Collective* – for game changers, thought leaders, rule breakers and style makers. Its overwhelmingly positive reception was truly humbling.

The point I'm making is that you never know where life is going to take you and the entrepreneur is always open to ideas and opportunities along the journey.

In 2007 I was asked to contribute a piece similar to this for a book published by the Australian Government, called "*Women Entrepreneurs: 18 Inspiring Tales of Small Business Success*". My thoughts now are essentially what they were then:

- Always think big.
- Create strategic alliances, aligning with corporations and those with a larger distribution network than yourself.
- Follow up and maintain relationships with the people you meet.
- Remember the importance of staff culture and team morale.
- Choose to surround yourself with people you like and who represent success to you. Success in your definition can mean all kinds of things.
- Find what it is that's holding you back, if you feel stuck. For me it was drinking and nine years ago I made the decision to quit. My life took off. I don't say you have to stop drinking – only to find what your roadblock is. It could be so-called friends, a partner, or a job that is draining. Just think about it.
- Always have new ideas on the go. Don't plan them from beginning to end before taking them to market – create a skeleton of your idea to gauge its interest factor. If no-one's interested, you've lost very little. If you're going to fail, fail quickly and move on to the next thing.

The most important advice I can give you is this – when you are really passionate about something, don't be disheartened by the naysayers. Believe in yourself and do whatever it is you set your mind to.

Lisa x

GO THE EXTRA MILE, IT'S NEVER CROWDED.

– Unknown –

Lorna Jane Clarkson

Founder and Chief Creative Officer, Lorna Jane

Move, Nourish, Believe

SO HOW DO I fit my words of wisdom into just 500 words?!

When I sit and think through my life, my own personal success and what has been the most important contributor to making my dreams a reality, it would have to be living actively with my Move, Nourish, Believe philosophy.

To me, moving and nourishing yourself every single day is vital for success. And when I talk about "Move", I don't just mean exercise; although I do think being physically fit is essential to think and be at your best. I'm also referring to the ability to keep moving forward in your life - learning, improving and getting closer to your goals.

When I say "Nourish", I am absolutely referring to giving your mind and body the nutrition it needs to have the consistent energy to strive for perfection every day. But I am also talking about nourishing your mind by reading inspiring words, and improving your knowledge both in business and in life. Travelling nourishes you by giving you unforgettable experiences to learn and grow from. So too does making the time to be peaceful so that you can think, readjust, fine-tune and be clear on where you are heading in your one precious life.

But the beginning and the driving force behind all of the success stories I know of would have to be "Believe" - having the belief that you can achieve whatever you want in your life and be willing to work for it. I know without a doubt that confidence in yourself and your abilities, together with a positive mindset, can transform an ordinary day into a magical one. And my life is proof that when you take one positive, magical day and repeat it over and over again, that dream you have been working towards will ultimately become a reality. Your life will be an active one, and everything that you have dreamed of.

Lorna Jane xx

ALL SUCCESSFUL PEO
ARE BIG DREAMERS. TH
FUTURE COULD BE, IDE
THEN THEY WORK EV
DISTANT VISION, TH
WHAT'S YOUR DREAM?
#LGBD #MYDREAM

LE MEN AND WOMEN
Y **IMAGINE** WHAT THEIR
IN EVERY RESPECT, AND
RY DAY TOWARD THEIR
GOAL OR **PURPOSE**.

– Brian Tracy –

Lucinda Barlow

Head of Marketing, Google Australia and New Zealand

1. THINK BIG

IN MY FINAL months before MBA graduation, a career advisor got me to do a visualisation exercise - rather than thinking about what I wanted to achieve in my career, she asked me to think what my ideal day at work would look like. A strong image came to mind – a meeting room filled with smart people, brainstorming a new consumer tech product to take to market. There was insight in this vision. I wanted a role that was collaborative, creative, technical, and user-focused.

Six months after I joined Symbian, I found myself sitting in a Finnish-designer boardroom, overlooking a frozen lake at Nokia House, Espoo, with a cross functional product and marketing team. We were creatively brainstorming the positioning of a new portfolio of smartphones. I suddenly thought, "Wow, this is it!", and then I realised, "This is it? I really should have thought much bigger than this!"

Thinking big is a core value at Google. It's something I've had to learn since I joined. It's uncomfortably exciting and incredibly enticing. Some people are born dreamers and big thinkers, while others need to be given permission to open their eyes and their ambitions. You can do this for yourself or your team by removing assumptions about today's world and asking simple "what if" questions. The wonderful thing is that it becomes easier to sell in a big idea than a small one. Big, audacious ideas attract the best people.

The natural partner to thinking big is failure. You have to be prepared to fail, to fail fast, to celebrate failure and to fail forward.

2. KNOW YOUR STRENGTHS AND FEED THEM

I'M A BIG BELIEVER in figuring out all the things you do best and getting even better at them. It's also liberating to identify your weaknesses and then ignore them. If the majority of your work and responsibility uses your strengths, you will love what you do and excel at it, you'll be a joy to work with and you will never feel like work is a chore.

3. HIRE THE BEST AND WORK AS A FAMILY

A GOOD SKILL TO LEARN is interviewing and hiring well. As a manager, it's the most important responsibility you have. In my experience, excellent team = bliss; average team = misery. Great people feed off each other and make a team zing. When you're hiring, don't compromise on your team. If you're not certain that a candidate is the best person for the job, that you couldn't work for this person one day, that you couldn't sit next to this person on a long-haul flight, do not hire them. Look instead for the smartest, most passionate person you can find. Passionate people bring their passion to work and bring others to their cause.

Your team members are the family that you choose. You will probably spend more time with your team than with your real family so make sure you choose well and create an open, honest culture where people can be themselves.

HAVE LESS,
DO MORE,
BE MORE.
– Unknown –

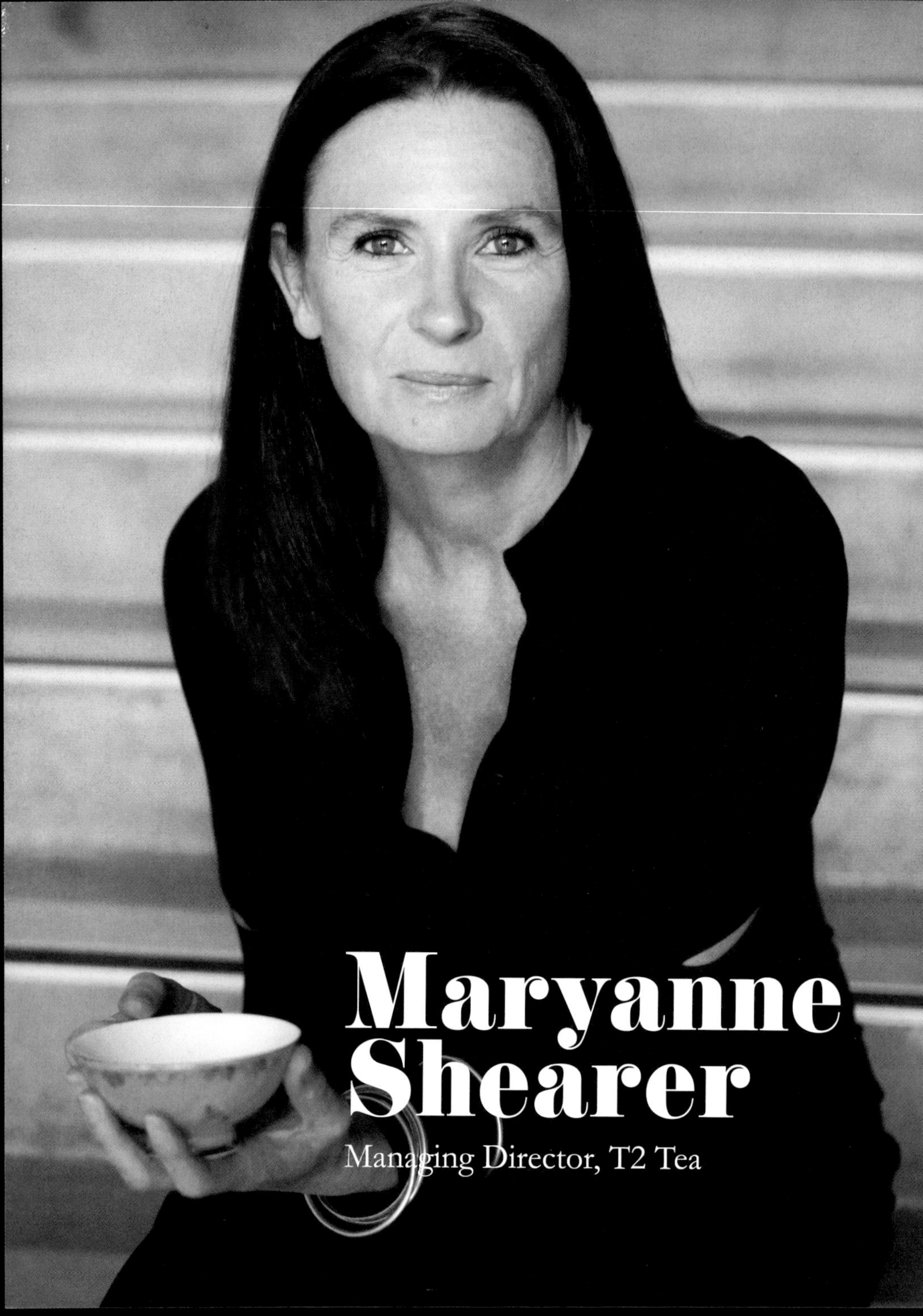
Maryanne Shearer
Managing Director, T2 Tea

I BELIEVE IN DOING WHAT YOU'RE GOOD AT AND IN DOING THINGS DIFFERENTLY.

IF YOU HAD TOLD ME when I was in my twenties, that one day I'd start a teashop and become a leading tea specialist, I would have laughed madly. I've loved fashion ever since I was a little girl and that's the industry I thought I would wind up in. I did start off there; I studied design and patternmaking after school. I went to Sydney and tried to find my way there as a designer, but that didn't work out. So, I came back to Melbourne and started working as a visual merchandiser and after that as a buyer for accessories. This was in the '80s when Madonna was over-accessorising and everyone stacked at least a dozen bangles on each arm, for any occasion. I started to buy collections for stores and styling photographic shoots. I moved to a much bigger brand and that was when I became very interested in the consumer psyche and how space is designed in a retail environment. Watching the successes and failures of products was incredibly exciting. I realised that if something wasn't working it could be reinvented.

My design, styling and buying experiences have gone to make up many of the skills I needed to create T2. All of the elements were there, I just hadn't thought of it yet. The idea didn't come until much later; in 1996, to be precise. I was having a chat with my business partner about the homewares business we had started four months earlier and how we couldn't get it to work. We thought a cup of tea would help us gather our thoughts. We brewed up a black tea and bang! That was it! Why don't we do tea? Everyone else is doing coffee; we could do tea. We went off in an excited frenzy and very soon after that we were putting Chinese wallpaper on the walls and painting the ceiling pink in our first store in Fitzroy, Melbourne. We decided our new company would be called Tea Too, but it was quicker to write T2. It was as simple as that.

Back then tea was an old, staid, stiff, gentleman's club kind of world. So we said, let's make it feminine, fun and fabulous and we changed everything. What do we do at T2? We love tea. That's what we do. We don't sell tea. We don't have a tea business. We just love tea and I think that's really important. We treat tea in a fashionable manner. We modernised it and took it to a different market. I never make a decision purely for the money. I will make an expensive decision because it's better for the brand and the customer and that's what sets us apart.

My advice is consistent; be open to any opportunity that comes your way and be courageous enough to make your dreams happen. I also believe in doing what you're good at, and in doing things differently. For me, if it was going to be tea, it had to be new tea; it had to be done differently. It was a fresh approach, and that's why T2 has been so successful. If you nurture your passion, you create your own opportunities. You can have an idea that can grow and evolve to become a reality - into a place you love going to each and every morning.

Image courtesy of T2 Tea

minds are
parachute

they only function
when they are open.

– Sir Thomas Dewar –

like

s...

SHARE WHAT INSPIRES YOU
#LGBD #INSPIRINGQUOTES

Megan Dalla-Camina

Director of Strategy, IBM
Author of *'Getting Real About Having It All'*

It has been a journey of passion, hard work and burnout, and ultimately, a story of learning to thrive.

I'VE BEEN BLESSED with having had a diverse career over the past twenty years that has taught me great lessons about business, about life and most importantly about myself. The work has been amazing. I've devised strategies for multibillion-dollar companies, been involved in global IPOs, completed a few Masters degrees and now a PhD, and worked at levels I only ever dreamed of all over the world. But it's the intersection with my personal journey where the real lessons are. It has been a journey of passion, hard work and burnout, and ultimately, a story of learning to thrive. I share a few gems from my path in the hope that they may shine a light on yours.

FIND YOUR PASSION

Nothing screams more loudly than passion. When you find the thing that moves you beyond all else, and you make that your life's work, you can create magic and thrive doing it. Go to whatever lengths you need to, to find your passion, and follow where it leads. Don't let others deter you from your path, from your calling. Only you know what it is and where it can take you.

GET CLEAR ON YOUR LIFE VISION

Don't make the mistake of thinking that life is all about work. Work is important, but it's only part of the puzzle. Get clear on what the holistic picture looks like for you. What are the elements you want in your life? Create that vision for yourself, put boundaries around it to protect it, and make that your reality.

VALUE YOUR UNIQUE EXPERTISE

You have unique strengths and experience that make what you have to offer valuable. Draw power and confidence from that. Work out what your strengths are, become as knowledgeable as you can in your chosen field, and keep learning and expanding. When you value yourself for the unique contribution that only you can make, other people will too.

BE PREPARED TO DO THE WORK

There is little you can't achieve when you make a commitment to do the work. People are always talking about hard work. You can reframe your thinking about that. I worked hard for a long time. But I know now that the work doesn't have to be hard. It just has to happen. When you work with grace and ease the results can be even better. That's where you will find your flow. And remember, nothing beats being prepared. Over prepared. Make it one of your core differentiators.

LOOK AFTER YOUR WELLBEING

When we are out making our way in the world, our wellbeing is often the last thing to get a look in. It needs to be the first. Learn to meditate. Get eight hours sleep. Move your body everyday. Nurture your relationships. Look at the stars and marvel at rainbows. And most importantly, tune into that inner knowing that will always tell you what you need to hear. You just need to get quiet enough to listen.

Megan Dalla Camina

SUCCESS
IS THE
SUM OF
SMALL
EFFORTS.
– Robert Collier –

GO
AT LEAST ONCE A
YEAR TO A PLACE
YOU HAVE
NEVER BEEN
BEFORE.

WHERE HAVE YOU NEVER BEEN?
#LGBD #NEWHEIGHTS

Melina Cruickshank

General Manager, Women's Networks Fairfax Media

Surround yourself with people who believe in your dreams.

IN MY WORKING LIFE the best advice I've received is that great careers take time to build. For me, building success is based on some core fundamentals - hard work, ambition and integrity.

Over the years I've evolved my leadership style through instinct and observation from all areas of the business. I've had plenty of informal mentors but I have a lot of women in my teams and they're all inspiring. The younger women coming up through digital media are smart and confident and they represent a new wave of feminism, where equality in the workplace is non negotiable.

In my career I've learnt you need to align yourself with positive individuals. I'm a big believer in attracting what you project. Corporate politics is inevitable but it's an individual decision on how you conduct yourself. And at the end of the day you need to stand for something.

I'm from a small country town in Victoria and always dreamt of a career in digital media. My mother worked incredibly hard to support me through university. She works in aged care and when I'm having a hard day, I remind myself of her. She is a positive woman who is grateful for such small things and loves it when I tell her about my world. There is a lot to be said about being grateful and I remind my teams we should appreciate our working environments as much as possible. Women before us fought so hard to allow choice and we should never, ever take it for granted.

YOUR LIFE
IS YOUR
MESSAGE
TO THE
WORLD
MAKE SURE
IT'S INSPIRING.
– Unknown –

In my 20s I was ambitious and worked very hard as digital was exploding. Living in London working for a digital agency I had various mentors who taught me enormous amounts about online, people and business. They were great days and really set up a strong foundation for me. In my 30's my life became a complete blur of managing work while taking the time to have my three children. There is no doubt it's tough and you need a great partner to make it work. My husband is that, and we continue to juggle through as a team.

I've been incredibly fortunate to work for progressive workplaces who allow flexibility. It's the key thing women need, particularly when they have small children. When children arrive, working parents have two full-time jobs and it's intense. Being a mother means my work represents different things to me now. You can have tough days but seeing my children's faces light up when I come home is incredible. It's a major reality check. I never, ever take that pure joy for granted. I've realised I'm a better mum and person when I work but you have to be happy in your work place to justify being away from your children.

The key theme I've had throughout my career is finding positive allies and informal mentors. My advice to young women now is to listen and observe as much as you can.

If you plan on having children find an employer who embraces flexibility because there is no way you can have work, children and happiness without that support from the workplace. And embrace women at work – support and help each other as much as possible. My women colleagues are brilliant for advice and a really good laugh.

Pip Marlow

Managing Director, Microsoft Australia

BE AUTHENTIC TO YOURSELF, KNOW YOUR TRUE NORTH AND HAVE SELF BELIEF.

TO KNOW ME is to know that I am passionate about my family. I have two absolutely amazing daughters and a brilliant husband. They are my first priority, my true north. That's why I'm very excited to be contributing to this piece of work. When complete, it's something that I'll give to my daughters because I'm a big believer in the sharing of wisdom between generations and the power of mentoring.

I deliberately use the words "between generations" because it's not all one way. A mentoring relationship is a two-way proposition and that's a little at odds with conventional practice. Traditionally, it's the older generation that's seen as the great giver of wisdom and the younger generation that receives it. Not entirely true. I have learnt as much from people who are younger than me as from people who are older than me. I learn new things from my daughters every day, and at work I speak with interns and graduates as much as with the senior leadership team. I passionately believe that it's vital to be open to all view points and that you treat every interaction with every person as an opportunity to learn and share wisdom. Workplaces have so much to gain when they embrace the 'wisdom of the crowd' but to do that they need an inclusive culture. Let me frame it like this: have you ever been in a workplace where you felt you couldn't be yourself? Where you couldn't find or add your full voice to a meeting, an idea, a plan or a conversation? Inclusiveness is about creating a culture where everyone can be themselves and where people can be their best. An inclusive culture enables diversity, and having a diverse workforce is great for business.

At Microsoft, we have over a billion customers in our Windows business alone and those customers come from a multitude of different cultures and backgrounds. We're a big believer that in order to serve our customers well, we need to mirror the market we serve. Perhaps the most obvious example is when you walk around Microsoft's offices, whether that be in Australia or our headquarters in Seattle. I'm always delighted to hear lots of different accents and to be constantly bumping

into people who hail from all corners of the planet. It's that diversity that helps us to understand our customers' needs and ensures that the products and services we bring to market satisfy and exceed those expectations. From this you can probably gather that I'm rather passionate about diversity and inclusion!

Being passionate is also really important to me. If you don't have a fire in the belly, then find it. As I said, I'm passionate about my family. I'm also passionate about what can happen when you bring the power of people together with big ideas, and the explosive achievement that can come from that. My proudest career moments have always come from a team achievement.

I also love Bill Gates' story. To me, he exemplifies someone who constantly has big, bold dreams and an unrelenting passion to change the world. I love that sort of energy and also the lesson that it imparts – that it's important to dream big, to have bold goals and to have the confidence and self-belief that you can do it. He did it and you can too.

While Bill Gates has obviously been incredibly successful, his journey and the story of Microsoft were not without some bumps. With big dreams there are also usually risks. Embracing risk is part of the innovation process as boundaries are pushed into the unknown. It's exciting and scary at the same time. The reality is that

sometimes it results in failure. As kids, we're taught that failure is a bad thing but I don't see it that way. If you never fail then you'll probably never push far enough or get outside of your comfort zone. The great thing about having bold goals is that if you aim for the stars and land on the moon, that's not a bad outcome!

Finally, don't be held back by your hardwired inhibitions. Ultimately in life there are going to be challenges that you can't control. The key is to focus on what you can control and spend less time on the things you can't. It's what's called the sticky floor trap – the things that can hold you back but that are within your power to control and change. Don't be a victim to the sticky floor.

On that note, a few parting words. I'm passionate about mentoring and helping all young people to reach their fullest potential. But I believe it's a particular responsibility for women in positions of leadership to be role models for other females. Why? On a personal level, it's for my daughters. Today, only three per cent of ASX 200 CEO positions are held by women but by the time my kids are in the workforce I want them to have an equal chance at achieving their full potential. You should have that opportunity too! Be authentic to yourself, know your true north and have self-belief. I guarantee it will take you an enormously long way.

Pip

WHY?

IF YOU WANT
TO GO FAST,
GO ALONE.
IF YOU WANT TO
GO FAR,
GO TOGETHER.

About

Little Girl Big Dream

Little Girl Big Dream is a passionate community committed to connecting and developing high calibre young professional women.

Aspiring to foster and flourish the careers of ambitious young women, Little Girl Big Dream offers high-quality networking platforms and professional development programs to empower and equip young women for success.

Through networking conferences, mentoring programs and leadership trainings, young women are given the opportunity to be inspired, supported and mentored by each other, as well as by some of Australia's most distinguished businesswomen and entrepreneurs.

Tailored for marketing, entrepreneurial and corporate professionals under the age of thirty-five, Little Girl Big Dream strives to raise awareness for women's need for development and provide learning opportunities and tools to facilitate career growth.

Our mission is to revolutionise the corporate landscape and nurture the next generation of female leaders.

"Never doubt that a small group of thoughtful, passionate and committed individuals can change the world. Indeed, it is the only thing that ever has."

– Margaret Mead –

How You Can Join The Movement

- Networking Conference
- The Think Tank Series
- Mentoring Program
- The Dream Collective Membership

#JoinLGBD

TESTIMONIALS

Stories of inspiration and transformation from our program participants.

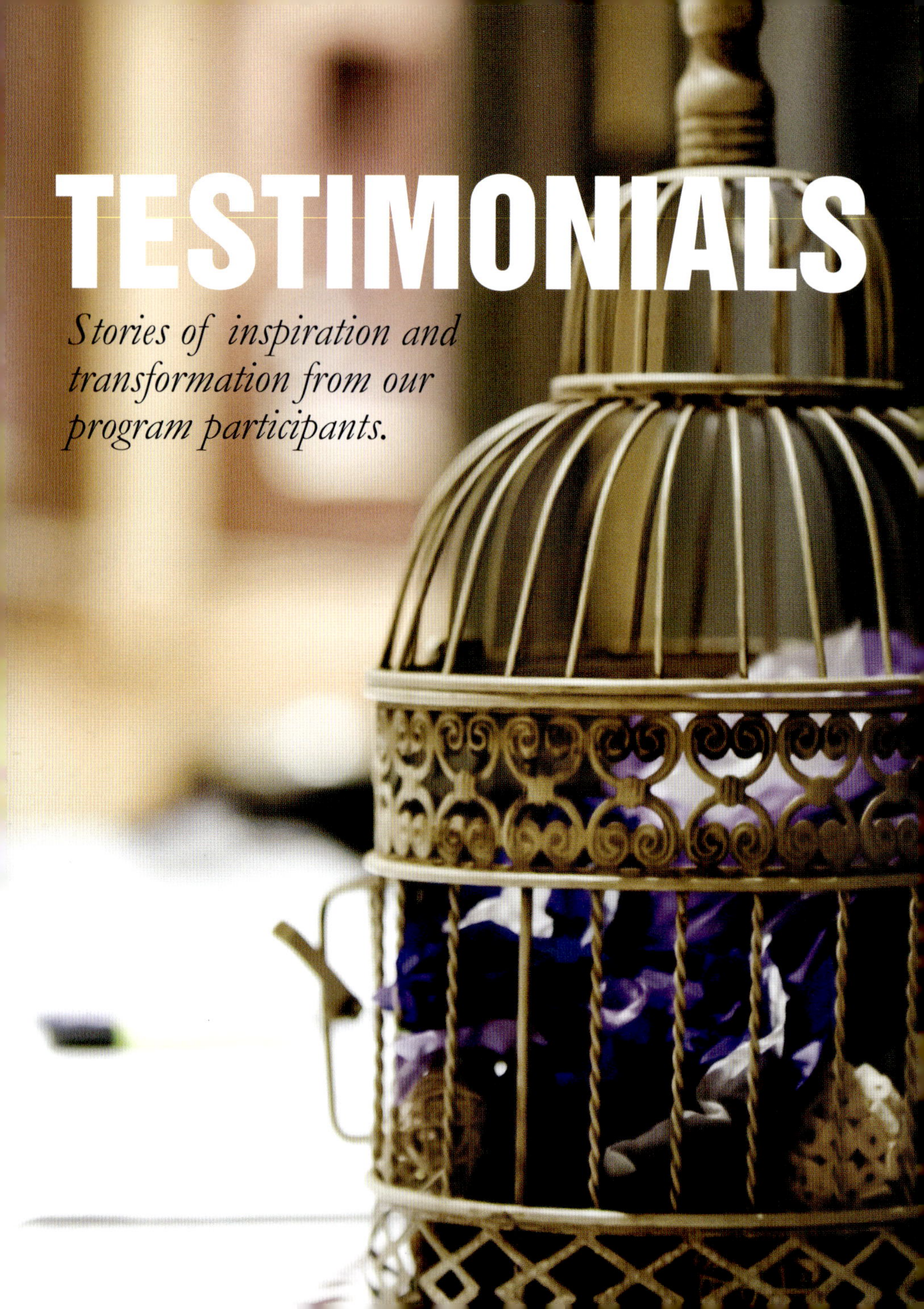

NETWORKING CONFERENCE

Jessica Montague

When I was growing up my mother taught me many valuable lessons. Looking back, two in particular stick in my mind. Firstly, that I could become anything I wanted to be. And secondly, as long as I did my best – and knew I'd put in 100 per cent – that was all that mattered.

But this wasn't all. The fact that my mother - a primary school teacher - often imparted such wisdom, taught me to listen to others. To respect and engage with those who'd achieved things before me. And to heed advice from older, wiser women.

I've been extremely fortunate that, since swapping my family's suburban enclave for the mad world of magazine journalism, I've experienced equally nurturing role models.

Magazine publishing is, quite frankly, a funny world. From the exterior it appears to be a world of the utmost luxury, full of soirées where champagne flows freely. In reality, though, I've seen girls who couldn't afford rent because their pay was so low and best friends who have experienced spectacular fall-outs all because they went for the same job.

The temptation of being swept away by the 'glamour' was intoxicating early on, but I've always been kept in check by grounded, senior 'sisters' who imparted advice akin to that of my mother.

Recently, my understanding of how crucial it is to learn from senior 'sisters' became more apparent. A year before *madison*'s closure in May 2013, I helped to launch madison mentors - a multi-platform initiative aimed at empowering professional women each month.

Through this I met Sarah Liu, founder of "Little Girl Big Dream". Sarah helped me tap into a pool of female business leaders willing to engage with younger women. While this served me well for stories, it had a far greater effect on me personally.

Ever since I attended Sarah's early conferences, I've been enthralled. Now that madison is sadly no longer in publication, there's not a reason for me to attend professionally. Instead, I attend of my own accord because each event leaves me inspired and with tools to make my goals a reality.

Through Little Girl Big Dream, I've also learned the true meaning of 'sisterhood'. I've learned there is a collective of generous women out there willing to pass on knowledge they've accumulated. I've learned we're all on the same team and it's our responsibility to help each other out.

This book is just another example of that. The fact all of these successful women have penned 500 Words of Wisdom for the next generation of female leaders is inspiring in itself.

And herein lies a sentiment I hope this book leaves you with. By all means, read each page and be captivated. But I urge you to also think about how you can perpetuate this cycle. How you can help to encourage younger females coming through.

Because as my mother taught me all those years ago, the most valuable gift you can give someone is the ability to dream big, and it's our responsibility to ensure the next generation coming through does just that.

Jessica is a Sydney-based freelance journalist and former features editor of madison *magazine.*

THE THINK TANK SERIES

Mariebelle Malo

During the last two years I had the chance to attend a few Little Girl Big Dream conferences. I was immediately impressed by the calibre of speakers, but even more by the group's common energy and the determination of all these young women in search of advice. I knew that surrounding myself with such company would directly evoke passion towards my own career. That is why I proposed to Sarah Liu to start The Think Tank Series, to recreate the conferences frequently and in a more intimate format.

The Think Tank quickly became my monthly breath of fresh air when I left my busy work schedule behind to invest in personal development. Surrounded by a handful of liked-minded women, we shared our aspirations and discussed different subjects we felt were important to our careers, progression and goals. Prior to the meetings, we all read and dissected thought-provoking articles and videos in relation to the evening's topic. We then invited expert guests to share their experiences and give personal perspectives on our unique situations.

The Think Tank has proven to be extremely useful in my day-to-day work. Every month I learned and applied new concepts ultimately aiming towards my own personal goals. For example, during one of the sessions we discussed the attributes of a great leader. I realised a great leader is also a great follower. Don't wait to be told! Bring solutions, anticipate the trend and more importantly be loyal to your manager. Helping them achieve their goal proved to be the best career advice I've ever received.

One of my favourite and most challenging sessions was to describe my brand and unique selling point. With the help of Think Tank pre-read material, I spent time defining my strengths. Once the draft was complete, I communicated my brand to the team and refined it based on their feedback. From this exercise I understood the attributes I wanted to be known for and those I needed to improve on to fully represent my brand.

These sessions made me realise the importance of developing my communication and leadership skills to progress my career. They encouraged me to find the right mentor, guided me in future decisions and made me challenge myself.

More than ever, The Think Tank Series pushed me to always produce the best within myself. It provided me with the opportunities to develop relationships with amazing women working in varying industries but sharing the same passion to succeed.

Thank you Sarah Liu for bringing The Think Tank Series to life. You are a role model to me and you will no doubt influence many great future women leaders.

Mariebelle is a Shopper Engagement Executive at Unilever Australia.

MENTORING PROGRAM

Monique Giron

Last year I was lucky to be involved with the LGBD mentor program, which included spending time with a mentor (even going to work with her for a day), attending the LGBD networking events and completing training days with the other mentees. My mentor was a highly experienced and successful business woman, wife and mother, who kindly took the time out of her very busy schedule to mentor me – for which I am very grateful.

I had never had a mentor before, but I gained so much from the experience – it's hard to know how to summarise it in 500 words! My mentor was a role model, a confidant, a teacher, an advisor and a friend. Spending time with her and being part of the program has really given me the confidence, courage and skills to keep pursing my dream – growing our business. In the last year our revenue has almost doubled and I don't know if we could have done it without my mentoring program. The program helped me to stay motivated and on track throughout the year – now the challenge is finding something similar this year!

I really valued the very open relationship I had with my mentor. She encouraged me to discuss anything I wanted to and so I did! We talked about everything from managing my emotions, managing staff, to having a good relationship with my husband and other family members. My business partner is my mother, which is a bit unique but it has worked well for us. So having a mentor who is a similar age to my mother, and who has a daughter who is a similar age to me, gave me new perspectives and a different outlook on issues. She also got me thinking a lot about what is really important and meaningful to me – a process which actually took the whole year because I am not such a deep thinker – but I got there eventually.

I also really valued the time I spent with the other mentees during the training and at the networking events. I was more than happy to travel all the way from Perth to Sydney to participate in all the different activities. In other circles, I often feel like the odd one out because I am so passionate about business and entrepreneurship. I found starting my own business a long and lonely journey, even with a business partner. But it was so inspiring to meet other women who are also passionate about business and their careers! Women who are going through the same things as I am, and who are working towards their dreams. Listening to the speakers at the various events also helped me broaden my horizons and inspired me to keep living my dream. I took courage and inspiration from these amazing women doing great things with their careers.

And lastly, like most women, I find that talking and sharing with other women is therapeutic in itself. So being able to share my journey with my mentor and the other mentees has been an amazing opportunity and has taught me so much! I am incredibly grateful to Sarah for setting up the program. Sarah's passion and dedication for encouraging young business women to follow their dreams is amazing, and the best part is that it's contagious! I can't wait to see what she has planned next!

Monique is a young entrepreneur and manager of Alecto Medical Recruitment.

Our Programs & Offerings

NETWORKING CONFERENCE

Little Girl Big Dream holds quarterly conferences for young professional women with a focus on Marketing, Entrepreneurship and Corporate leadership.

The networking conferences offer a unique opportunity to hear industry-leading speakers share their insight, expertise and journey to success. This is also an effective forum to connect like-minded women who share the same drive and passion for career advancement.

THE THINK TANK SERIES: CAREER WORKSHOP

The Think Tank Series is a monthly 90-minute professional development workshop to connect and advance high potential young women.

The Think Tank Series is a forum where passionate young women come together and share learning, resources and insights relevant to their respective industries. The Think Tank Series encourages collaboration through facilitated discussion, debate and skills training. Members are encouraged to set and track goals attainment as part of the program to drive and ensure progress.

MENTORING PROGRAM

A good mentor's wisdom will shape your future and reveal to you your own riches.

The Little Girl Big Dream Mentoring Program is an exclusive ten-month program offered to selected young women with the desire to further their careers within three identified categories:

- Marketing
- Entrepreneurship
- Corporate Leadership

The program matches young professionals with successful and highly established role models who, through one-on-one mentoring sessions, can assist with the mentees' career and business progression. Spaces are highly limited and mentees will be selected through a rigorous application, interview and matching process.

THE DREAM COLLECTIVE MEMBERSHIP

Becoming a member of THE DREAM COLLECTIVE is really something special. It is your opportunity to embark on a journey that brings about transformation and advancement to your career and business. Experience growth, support and collaboration like never before. Benefits of the membership include, exclusive access to business resources and intelligence; discounted rates and special offers; member only career/business coaching with high profile business leaders; VIP events and annual retreat.

Visit us:

www.littlegirlbigdream.com

Connect with us:

facebook.com/myLGBD

twitter/Sarahliu

Contact us:

sarah@littlegirlbigdream.com

4

Raves...

"Little Girl Big Dream is a fabulous association. The network of professional members and guest speakers is extremely inspiring and motivational. Little Girl Big Dream provides the opportunity to meet like minded, driven women through well executed, enjoyable events."

"Little Girl Big Dream has been a great networking opportunity for me. I am able to share my experiences and learn from others."

"Just want to tell you that event was very good and very insightful. I feel like I'm looking at my career differently now. Would love to attend the conference again!"

"Little Girl Big Dream offers a great opportunity for young women to invest in their professional development. LGBD's seminars facilitate exposure to a diverse group of senior businesswomen sharing their experiences and provides high quality networking opportunities."

"It is a wonderful experience meeting like-minded young professional women. Little Girl Big Dream inspires all the girls who have a dream to go for it."

"The Little Girls Big Dreams Association is a wonderful initiative a group focusing on younger women in the workforce, offering high quality networking and opportunities to unite, connect and be inspired by each other and senior business professionals."

"A fantastic forum to encourage, inspire and provide great advice to young professional women!"

"Little Girl Big Dream is the perfect association for young professional women wanting to connect, communicate and most importantly, learn from contemporaries."

"A great way to meet young professionals genuinely passionate about their careers."

"Thank you for hosting such a wonderful event! The speakers were all truly inspiring in their different ways, and it truly was a case of little girl, big dreams and how they have achieved them."

"LGBD empowers women and gives them the opportunities to shine."

"I believe it s really important for young professional women to nurture supportive business relationships and the Little Girl Big Dream network is a great environment in which to establish these connections."

Be BOLD
or
Italic,
but never
REGULAR
– Unknown –

About Sarah

SARAH IS A branding specialist and an entrepreneur, but nothing describes her better than a little girl with a big dream.

Ever since a young age, she's had "I'm a little girl with a big dream" written on her bedroom wall. But rather than dreaming of living in a castle, winning the lottery or marrying a prince, Sarah's dream has always been about helping people achieve excellence and create positive influence in the world.

We all know what growing up is like; trying to secure the next promotion, getting that much deserved pay rise and climbing that corporate ladder. Sarah was no different. She left her dream behind as soon as she entered the corporate world. Until she was selected into a mentoring program for marketing women, she met many ambitious young women like herself, who shared the desire for learning and success yet were confronted with the lack of support available in the corporate world. She was disappointed to see the lack of recognition of young women's need to be mentored and the limited resources available to facilitate career growth for professional women with high potential.

That's when her dream was ignited once again.

She took it upon herself to create a supportive network that empowers young women to pursue their dreams and equip them with the skills necessary for success. She founded Little Girl Big Dream in 2011, while juggling a demanding full time job and a small business on the side. She had no financial support, no business partner, no resources and few contacts. But what she had in abundance was the passion to unite ambitious young women, help them achieve their career goals and develop them as competent leaders in their respective industries.

The birth of Little Girl Big Dream is the realisation of Sarah's dream. Nothing excites Sarah more than seeing her business flourish; inspiring young women to reach their full potential, developing them into confident and capable business leaders, and driving change in the corporate world.

OUR AM
CONTRIB

AZING
UTORS

Image courtesy of kikki K

Amy Smith

Amy Smith has a long and successful background in advertising as the CEO of JWT UK, Australia & New Zealand, before becoming the CEO of Jenny Craig in 2008. Amy doubled the business in five years and in April 2013 left to establish Rise Productions, a marketing and brand strategy consultancy. She continues to be a passionate advocate in championing women in business.

Carolyn Creswell

Carolyn Creswell is the founder of Carman's Fine Foods, which celebrates its twentieth birthday this year and has a strong following in more than thirty-two countries around the world. Carolyn has grown Carman's to become the number one selling muesli brand on Australian supermarket shelves and was named the 2012 Telstra Australian Business Woman of the Year.

Catriona Noble

Catriona Noble was the youngest female restaurant manager in McDonald's history and has since risen through the ranks to her current role as Chief Executive Officer of McDonalds Australia. She is also one of five female members of the Business Council of Australia, and last year was added to the nation's Who's Who.

Catriona Watson -Lamb

Catriona is the General Manager of Global Marketing and Communications at Bendon Group - one of the world's leading intimate apparel companies for brands including Elle Macpherson Intimates, Stella McCartney Lingerie, Lovable and Bendon. Prior to Bendon, Catriona has had a successful marketing career in roles such as Head of Marketing at Revlon UK and National Marketing Manager Estee Lauder.

Gillian Franklin

Gillian Franklin is the Founder and Managing Director of The Heat Group Pty Ltd, the largest Australian owned personal care company. A vision to develop and market brands specifically for a new generation of women is what drove Gillian to start Heat in May 2000. The Heat Group now exclusively distribute leading global brands including Max Factor, COVERGIRL, Bourjois, Essence and Jeanne Arthes fragrances. She is the owner and distributor of ulta3, MUD Make Up Design, and Billie Goat Soap, and is an official licensee of Warner Bros personal care products.

Ghazaleh Lyari

After a long-term and extremely successful career as a Wall Street Investment Banker, Ghazaleh Lyari put her passion for cupcakes and years of business knowledge into practice with the launch of Ghermez Cupcakes, offering its customers an "extraordinary culinary and retail experience".

Jacinta Tynan

Jacinta Tynan is a news presenter with Sky News Australia, an author, columnist and actor, who also appears regularly on Sunrise and The Morning show as a commentator. She is also a patron of SISTER2Sister, a mentor program for disadvantaged teenage girls.

Jackie Frank

Jackie Frank has forged an extremely successful and high-profile career in the world of women's magazines. She has been editor of *marie claire* magazine since its launch eighteen years ago, and in 2005 was made the first Australian Publisher of the prestigious magazine. She is one of Australia's most respected magazine editors.

Jane Huxley

Jane Huxley is the CEO of Pandora in Australia and New Zealand. Pandora is a free, personalised radio service, used daily by tens of millions of people, and the best job of her life! Prior to this, she spent five years at the helm of Digital for Fairfax Media and has more than twenty years of leadership experience in digital media, technology and consumer markets.

Janine Allis

Janine Allis is the founder and Managing Director of Boost Juice. From a housewife with no formal business training to a phenomenon entrepreneur, Janine's success in turning a single juice bar into a global company with more than 6,000 employees and $160 million in global sales led to her recognition as Telstra Business Woman of the Year.

Janine Garner

Janine Garner is the Founder and Director of LBDG, which is a business and support network for women who want to succeed on their own terms. She was previously Group Marketing Director of the OrotonGroup and was instrumental in the rejuvenation of the Oroton brand and the elevation of Ralph Lauren in the Asia-Pacific region. Her passion is "practical philanthropy and equal opportunity for all who strive for success".

Jayne Hrdlicka

Jayne Hrdlicka BA, MBA, has been Chief Executive Officer of Jetstar Group since July 1, 2012, and is currently a Non-Executive Director at Woolworths Ltd. Prior to this, Jayne was Group Executive of Strategy and Information Technology of Qantas Airways Limited. She has also previously served as a senior partner at Bain & Company, and was an Executive in the publishing and marketing industry.

Kim Lion

Kim is the Managing Director of Universal McCann Australia (UM) in Melbourne. UM is recognised as Australia's highest ranked and most awarded media agency, amongst the five largest in Australia, with annual media billings in excess of AU$800 million. Kim is a member of UM's national board, and prior to this role served as UM's National Chief Client Officer.

Kristina Karlsson

By combining her appreciation of Swedish design with her love of stationery, Kristina 'Kikki' Karlsson founded kikki.K Swedish Home/Office Style. Today, she is the Founder and Creative Director of the company, which has over 80 boutiques in Australia, New Zealand, Singapore, and an online store that services the world.

Larke Riemer

Larke Riemer is the Director Women's Markets for Westpac and is also the Global Ambassador for the Global Banking Alliance for Women, whose mission is to accelerate the growth of women in business and women's wealth creation globally. Larke was recognised for her efforts in advancing economic empowerment of women worldwide and was awarded with the World of Difference award by The International Alliance for Women.

Layne Beachley

Layne Beachley is widely regarded as the most successful female surfer in history. She is the only surfer, male or female, to claim six consecutive world titles (1998 to 2003). Layne has also established the Layne Beachley Aim For The Stars Foundation, helping young women achieve their goals. Layne also serves on the board of Surfing Australia and Sport Australia Hall Of Fame, among other prominent roles.

Lisa Messenger

Lisa Messenger is the Editor-in-Chief of the newest and most inspirational magazine to hit the newsstands, *Renegade Collective.* She is also the Owner and Creative Director of The Messenger Group and has for years worked globally in events, sponsorship, marketing, PR and publishing.

Lorna Jane Clarkson

Lorna Jane Clarkson, Founder and Chief Creative Officer of Australia's leading activewear label for women, Lorna Jane, stitched her first activewear design over 20 years ago. Today, Lorna Jane has evolved into something so much more than activewear. The brand is guided by Lorna's personal philosophy of Move, Nourish, Believe; empowering women worldwide to get fit, improve their health, and achieve great things through Active Living.

Lucinda Barlow

Lucinda leads Google's marketing efforts to bring Google products to Australian and New Zealand users and help more businesses grow online. She brings over 13 years experience working in Internet and mobile in Asia, the US and UK. Before joining Google, Lucinda was VP Marketing Communications for Symbian where she led a global team promoting smartphone technology.

Maryanne Shearer

Maryanne Shearer is the founder and Managing Director of T2. T2 offers Australia's largest range of loose-leaf tea and teawares. With T2, Maryanne opened up a world of tea that Australians had never seen before, and created a design-conscious retail experience to house that world. This innovation and success has also won her the 2012 Australian Veuve Clicquot Business Woman Award.

Megan Dalla-Camina
Having spent close to 20 years working for large multi-national companies such as GE, PwC and IBM, Megan is now the Director of Strategy at IBM and the author of *Getting Real About Having It All* (Hay House). She is a strategist, coach and speaker, and a passionate advocate for empowering women in business. Her inspiring leadership saw her awarded the 2013 NAB Women's Agenda Emerging Leader in the Private Sector Award.

Melina Cruickshank
Melina Cruickshank is the General Manager of Fairfax Women's Network, which is a collection of nine brands – reaching a monthly audience of more than 2.75 million women visitors. Melina has extensive experience in all aspects of the digital industry with a particular focus in online commercial strategy and execution.

Pip Marlow
Born and raised in New Zealand, mother of two Pip Marlow began her career with Microsoft in the Australian partner team in 1995 and subsequently spent eight years in various senior roles in the company's head offices in Seattle, USA. She returned to Australia in 2004, and in 2011 was appointed to the role of Managing Director of Microsoft Australia.

If you can dream it,
you can do it.

– Walt Disney –

Image courtesy of kikki K

THE SECRET: KEEP GOING

WHAT ARE SOME OF YOUR SUCCESS TIPS?
#LGBD #SECRETSFORSUCCESS

Acknowledgement

The most heartfelt and sincere thanks goes out to everyone who's supported me so generously on this journey. To the most amazing team one can wish for – Stellina, Annie, Cora & Shamagne, thank you for all that you have done for me and LGBD. This wouldn't have been possible without you.

A huge thanks to Jessica Montague, Mariebelle Malo and Monique Giron for contributing your testimonials.

To the PR genius Nikki Hunt from Think PR & Events, thank you for sharing my vision and your relentless work to make this book the success it is.

My hat off to the supremely talented Jimmy Tsang from Jimmy Tsang Photography; thank you for your creativity, online expertise, unwavering support and enduring all the endless late nights! Thanks to Simon from SW Photography for all your support and amazing work throughout the past years. Also a special thanks to my brother Dawson, for being the best legal counsel.

To all the lovely girls from The Messenger Group, thank you for holding my hand through this daunting process and for such a beautiful book!

To everyone from our LGBD network for making Little Girl Big Dream the passionate and excellent forum it is today.

To GW – Thank you for everything. You're my source of strength, inspiration and the reason why I can do what I do.

To every single one of our contributors, sponsors and partners who believe so much in me and what I do. Thank you.

This belongs to all of us.